SERVING

in the Meetings & in the Gospel

Witness Lee

Living Stream Ministry
Anaheim, California

First Edition, May 2000.

ISBN 0-7363-0909-8

Published by

Living Stream Ministry
2431 W. La Palma Ave., Anaheim, CA 92801 U.S.A.
P. O. Box 2121, Anaheim, CA 92814 U.S.A.

Printed in the United States of America

00   01   02   03   04   05   /   9   8   7   6   5   4   3   2   1

CONTENTS

PREFACE

This book is composed of messages given by Brother Witness Lee in Los Angeles, California in the winter of 1964. These messages were not reviewed by the speaker.

CHAPTER ONE

WORSHIPPING IN SPIRIT AND IN TRUTHFULNESS

Scripture Reading: John 4:20-24

In these messages we will consider the proper Christian service. This is a big subject that covers many matters. We will be concerned not merely with messages, teachings, doctrine, and knowledge. Rather, we will deal with practice and experience.

The service actually includes all Christian activities. We do not use the word *service* in the same way that Christianity does. Service also includes how to have the meetings. In Christian service and activity the first and most important thing is to meet, to have meetings. Without meeting it is impossible to have the Christian service or any kind of Christian activity. In other words, all Christian service and activities depend on meeting. Therefore, the first thing we must learn is how to meet.

The genuine Christian meeting is not a meeting like that in today's Christianity. Meetings in Christianity today are according to the system of the clergy and the laity. I hope that we would not have *clergy* and *laity* in our dictionary. We have to drop these two words. We have no such distinction. We are all priests; we believe in the universal priesthood. For us to come together means that all the members, not only a few responsible brothers, need to share the responsibility of the meeting. In the meetings, strictly speaking, there are no responsible brothers. All are simply brothers. When we come together, we come on the same standing with the same status. When we meet, we share the responsibility in the meetings.

In these messages we will also consider how to reach

people, how to have an outreach, that is, how to preach the gospel to the unbelievers. We must learn how to bring Christ to the unbelievers and also how to contact believers. We also need to learn how to help people in life. This needs much practice. It involves knowing how to minister life to people and how to help them go on in the spiritual life.

WORSHIPPING GOD IN OUR HUMAN SPIRIT

First, we must see the basic principle for our service, work, and activities. When we speak about service, work, and activities, we need to remember well what the Lord taught us in John 4. Verses 23 and 24 say, "But an hour is coming, and it is now, when the true worshippers will worship the Father in spirit and truthfulness, for the Father also seeks such to worship Him. God is Spirit, and those who worship Him must worship in spirit and truthfulness." In these verses, the word *spirit* is not capitalized. This is very important. Many people know this verse, but most understand that *spirit* here is the Holy Spirit. The thought in today's Christianity is that we worship in the Holy Spirit. This is not wrong, but what is more basically important is that in the New Testament time we must learn how to worship God in our human spirit. This has been neglected very much in Christianity. It is rather hard to find a message that tells us that we have to worship and serve God in our human spirit.

WORSHIPPING GOD IN TRUTHFULNESS

In addition, many may think that truthfulness as mentioned in John 4 is teaching or doctrine. Others say that truthfulness here means sincerity, that we must worship God with sincerity. Neither of these is accurate. Truthfulness here does not refer to mere doctrine or sincerity. Because God is Spirit, it is easy, logically speaking, to understand that we must worship God in spirit. But it is more difficult to understand why we must worship Him in truthfulness.

Why must we worship God, who is Spirit, in truthfulness? In order to understand a portion of Scripture, we first need its context. The context of these two verses gives us the background. This is the word which the Lord Jesus spoke to the Samaritan woman. That woman raised the problem of worship, saying, "Our fathers worshipped in this mountain, yet you say that in Jerusalem is the place where men must worship" (v. 20). The background of the word spoken here is the worship in the Old Testament. Therefore, we must see what the worship in the Old Testament was.

Worshipping on the Unique Ground

There were two main matters related to the worship in the Old Testament. According to Deuteronomy 12 to 16, the first main item was the place appointed by God as the center of worship, which eventually was Jerusalem. All the worshippers of God in the Old Testament time had to go to Jerusalem, to the very spot chosen and appointed by God. This kept the oneness of the people of Israel. No Israelite had any right to set up another place as a center for worship. If they would have had that right, it would have been too easy to have divisions. The unique, central place was the very factor which kept the unity of the people of Israel for all their generations.

Throughout thousands of years on this earth there has always been only one temple; there have never been two. All the people of Israel knew that no one had the right to choose any other place as a ground, a site, to raise up a temple. Even if they built a temple in Babylon exactly the same in size, shape, and material as the one Solomon built in Jerusalem, it would not have been the real temple, because it was not on the right ground. The right ground was the very factor that kept the oneness of the people of God.

According to Deuteronomy 12 to 16, the people had the right to enjoy every kind of produce of the good land of Canaan, but when they were going to enjoy that produce for the worship to God, they had no right to do it in any place other than the unique place, Jerusalem. This is God's wisdom to keep the oneness. Later on, after the captivity, the Jewish people had many synagogues, but they never dared to have a second temple.

Worshipping with the Riches of the Good Land

The second main item related to worship was all the

types in the Old Testament. We need much time to learn the types. There were many types. The most basic one was the good land of Canaan into which the people of Israel were brought, which typifies Christ into whom the people of God today have been brought. This refers us to Genesis 1:9-10, in which on the third day of creation God brought the dry land out of the water of death. This signifies the resurrection of Christ; Christ as the land buried under the death water was raised on the third day. Out of that land came many different lives—the vegetable life, the animal life, and the human life, which is in the likeness of God. This typifies that all life comes out of the resurrected Christ. Later this land became the good land of Canaan, which God prepared for His people. In this way, the people of Israel being brought into the good land typifies that we today have been brought into Christ, who is our good land.

After being brought into the good land, the people of Israel lived in the land, by the land, and with the land. They walked in it, moved in it, worked in it, and did everything in it. They obtained their food, their clothing, and their dwelling place from this land. They had everything for their living from the land. This also is a type, typifying that Christ is everything to us. We have to walk in Him, do things in Him, move in Him, and live in, live by, and live with Him. We also obtain our food, clothing, and dwelling place from Him. All that we need is in Christ.

There is a saying that a picture is better than a thousand words. For this reason, I like the Old Testament more than the New Testament. Many people say that the New Testament is better, but in a sense the Old Testament is better than the New, because as young children we need a "kindergarten" that teaches with pictures. If we tell a little child about a dog, he may not know what a dog is, but if we show him a picture of a dog, he will right away understand. We need the Old Testament to show us the pictures. We need to spend time to meditate and pray about the good land and how much the good land meant to the people of Israel. Everything they needed came out of the good land. The record of the good land speaks of many things, including vegetables, animals, minerals such as brass and iron, mountains, rivers, and springs. From these unsearchable riches of the good land the people of God received all that they needed.

Whenever the people of God came to worship God, they were commanded not to come with their hands empty. They had to come with their hands full of the surplus of the produce of the good land. We use the word *surplus* because the people of Israel put aside a certain portion of their produce from the good land for the purpose of God's worship. We usually think of this portion as a tithe of one-tenth, but if we study Leviticus through Deuteronomy carefully, we find that the people put aside at least three portions of one-tenth (Deut. 16:16). They had to put aside one-tenth, another tenth, and another tenth of the produce they obtained from the good land, not for their own living but for the purpose of worshipping God. In this way, whenever they came together to worship God they brought a surplus of the produce of the good land to God.

Our Need to Labor on Christ as Our Good Land

The surplus of the produce of the good land typifies Christ, and the way to have the surplus is to labor on Christ. Regrettably, some brothers and sisters are lazy. D. L. Moody, who throughout his life brought myriads of people on two continents to Christ, said that he never saw a lazy person get saved. Perhaps he was too extreme to say this, but I can say that I have never seen a lazy person who could be spiritual. A lazy person may be saved, but I am sure that he cannot be spiritual. You can be brought into the good land, but if you are lazy, you will have no surplus. Rather, you will be a beggar. If we are diligent and industrious to labor on the land God allotted to us, we will have much produce from this rich land. This produce will be enough not only for us to live on but also for us to have a surplus.

The surplus is the first tenth, not the last tenth. The Israelites had to separate every first lamb and every first tenth of the produce for the Lord. This typifies that after being brought into Christ, we need to labor on Christ, to cooperate with the Holy Spirit to live by Christ. Some may say that we should not use the word *labor* because today is the dispensation of grace; they say everything is of grace, not of works. There is no doubt that the good land given to us is a grace. The sunshine, the air, the early rain, and the latter rain are also a grace. However, we still have to till the ground. We cannot say that grace will till the ground for us; grace will never do that. From the very beginning of the Scriptures, after Adam was created, man had to till the ground. We need to till the ground, sow the seed, and reap the harvest. Grace will not do these things for us. We cannot bring rain down from heaven. That is not our ability; that is something beyond our ability. That is truly something of grace. Sunshine, air, rain, and the rich soil are all of grace. However, we must realize that we all have our responsibility.

Every morning we have to rise up early. Not one farmer can be lazy; every one has to rise up early in the morning. If we do not rise early in the morning to spend a little time with Christ, I am certain that when we come to the meeting, we will have nothing in our hand. We will come to the meeting with empty hands. We need to rise up a little earlier, contact the Lord, read the Word, and pray a little to till the ground, sow the seed, and reap the harvest. Some may say that we should not be legalistic in this way. However, we need to be legalistic three times a day in order to eat. We can fast only for a while; if we fast all the time, we will not be able to live.

Day by day we must rise up early to spend some time with the Lord; this is our labor. We have to pray; this is our labor. We also have to exercise our spirit to contact the Lord throughout the whole day; this also is our labor. Moreover, we must deal with many enemies, including the flesh, the self, and the environment. Even our family, friends, relatives, neighbors, colleagues, classmates, and roommates are problems we have to deal with. We also have to preach the gospel and learn to help others. All these are items of the labor we should have. If we labor in all these ways, we will have the rich produce of Christ our good land. Then when we come to the meeting, we will come with our hands full of the riches of Christ. Because day and night we labor on Christ, we will have a rich produce that is not only good enough for us to live in Christ and by Christ, but also good enough for us to come to worship God. In this way, when we come to God, we come with Christ.

As we have seen, there were two main items related to the worship in the Old Testament: the central place and all the types. If you spend time to read the Scriptures, the Holy Spirit will lead you to understand the background of the worship in the Old Testament. Based on this, the Lord told the Samaritan woman, "An hour is coming." This means that at the time the Lord spoke this word, the age, the dispensation, had changed. Before that time was the old age, the old dispensation, in which there was the worship of the Old Testament. Now, however, the age has changed. Now the proper worship, the true worship, is not a matter of a place or of the types. It is a matter in the spirit, not of Jerusalem, and it is a matter in truthfulness, not of the types. The worship of the New Testament time is a worship in the spirit and a worship in truthfulness.

Worshipping with the Christ
Whom We Have Experienced

Along with the types there were also regulations, rules, and laws related to the worship in the Old Testament time. However, all those types, rules, and laws are only empty figures. They are not the reality, the truth. Now the age, the dispensation, has changed. God is seeking to have people who worship Him in spirit, not at Jerusalem, and in truthfulness, in reality, no longer in types and regulations.

We all know what our human spirit is, but what is the reality? The reality is Christ. All the offerings—the sin offering, the trespass offering, the peace offering, the burnt offering, and the meal offering—are types and shadows. Those things are not the reality. The reality of all the offerings is Christ Himself. Likewise, the reality of love for God and love toward our neighbors is Christ. Now there is no need to keep the laws and regulations. There is, however, the need for us to take Christ as our life and live by Him; then we will have the reality.

In the ancient times, people came to God with the produce

of the land. Now, in this New Testament time we come to God with the Christ whom we have experienced. In the ancient times, people also worshipped God by keeping the commandments, such as those concerning loving God and loving their neighbors. Today, however, we worship God not by keeping the commandments but by taking Christ as our life. When we take Christ as our life, Christ is love for us to love God, and Christ is love toward our neighbors. All those commandments are empty; they are not the truth, the reality. Today Christ is the reality.

OUR NEED TO EXERCISE OUR SPIRIT

If we realize the background of the Lord's word in John 4, we will know the proper meaning of worship. We must realize that worship today—our service, work, and activities—must be in the human spirit and in Christ as the reality. It must not be in forms, rules, or regulations. Throughout many generations, at least from the time of the Reformation almost five centuries ago, many devoted Christians have tried again and again to study the New Testament to find the proper way for Christians to worship God. However, no one could find the answer. I myself did the same thing, and I could not find the answer. Eventually I found that the principle is to worship in spirit and in reality.

Sometimes dear brothers ask me if it is best to begin our meeting with a hymn. I say that this is perhaps right but not absolutely right. It depends on whether the hymn is called and sung in the spirit. If the hymn is called and sung in a formal way as a ritual, it is wrong. Some brothers ask if it is right to have hymns first and then prayers. I reply that this is fine if it is in the spirit. However, it may not be in the spirit; it may be done according to a program, not a program printed on paper but one printed in our mind. In this case, it is wrong. We all have to learn how to exercise our spirit.

The exercise of our spirit is one of the items of the Lord's recovery in these last days. To worship in the human spirit has been much neglected by today's Christianity. Many today have forgotten about the exercise of the human spirit and instead exercise their mind. Therefore, in order to be trained in a proper way in the Lord's service in the church life, the first matter is that we must learn to exercise our spirit. We may compare exercising our spirit for our service to using our feet to play soccer. When I was a young boy, I was fond of playing soccer, which we called *football*. Even in the classroom while I was listening to the lecture, I was exercising my feet, because I knew that after class we would go to play a game. In the United States, however, the game called "football" is played more with the hands than with the feet. To exercise our mind in the service is like using our hands to play soccer. We need to learn how to exercise our spirit.

We need to learn to exercise our spirit in our daily life. The Epistles tell us that we must walk according to the spirit (Rom. 8:4-6). The King James Version often uses *Spirit* with a capital letter in passages such as these, but the better translations render *spirit* with a small letter. To walk in spirit means to exercise our spirit by our daily walk. If we are exercised to walk according to the spirit, when we come to the meetings our spirit will be active. We will know how to exercise our spirit. How can I play football if I do not know how to exercise my feet? Many Christians simply do not know how to exercise their spirit, so when they come to the meeting, they do not know how to worship God in spirit.

In these days we cannot overstress this matter. We always should stress that we must help the brothers and sisters to learn how to exercise their human spirit. Even in our home, in dealing with our family, we must learn how to exercise our spirit, to do and speak things not by our mind, emotions, desires, or likes but by the inner feeling, the consciousness of the spirit. We must learn how to exercise according to the deepest feeling in our spirit. Then we will be used to exercising our spirit, so whenever we come to the meeting, we will be ready.

In order to play tennis, we have to exercise our wrist. When we are accustomed to exercising our wrist, we can play tennis, but if we do not exercise in this way, how can we play the game? In order to be trained in the church life, the first thing we must consider is the exercise of the spirit. We must learn how to worship God in our human spirit, because today God as the Spirit dwells in our spirit.

God is Spirit, and this divine Spirit dwells in our spirit. For this reason, the Epistles, particularly those of the apostle Paul, tell us that the Lord is with our spirit. There are many expositions of the book of Galatians, but it is hard to find one that speaks on the last verse of that book. At the end of Galatians, the last verse says, "The grace of our Lord Jesus Christ be with your spirit" (6:18). Regardless of how much we know the teachings of Galatians, if we do not know how to realize the grace of Christ in our spirit, we will not be able to have the experiences of Christ taught in this book. In the first four chapters of Galatians we have the teachings of Christ: Christ revealed in us (1:16), Christ living in us (2:20), Christ put on us (3:27), and Christ being formed in us (4:19). The last two chapters, however, deal with the spirit: walking by the Spirit (5:16, 25) and the grace of our Lord Jesus Christ being with our spirit (6:18). All the teachings about Christ must be applied in our spirit; then we will have the experience of Christ.

We must learn how to discern our spirit and to exercise it all the time. Then whenever we come together, we will know how to use our spirit. Our spirit will be on the alert, ready, active, and living. If we do not learn to exercise the spirit, we will not be able to have the proper church life. The church life is a life in the human spirit with the indwelling Holy Spirit. The Holy Spirit today indwells our spirit, so we must know how to exercise our spirit. This is one aspect of the principle of the New Testament worship.

COMING TOGETHER TO EXHIBIT CHRIST

As we have seen, the other aspect of the New Testament worship is to worship in truthfulness, that is, in reality, in Christ. When we come to the meetings, we have to exercise our spirit, but what should we exercise to do in our spirit? The people in the ancient times had to bring all their surplus to Jerusalem to offer it and enjoy it with one another in the presence of God. At least a part of what they offered was food to God. Not only the people of Israel enjoyed the surplus, but

God also enjoyed it. This typifies that we come to the meetings to exercise our spirit to exhibit Christ. When the people of Israel came together and brought all their surplus to Jerusalem, that became a "fair," an exhibition, of the produce of the good land. Likewise, when we Christians come together, the Christian meeting is an exhibition of Christ. We exercise our spirit to exhibit Christ.

LABORING ON CHRIST TO HAVE A SURPLUS OF CHRIST

We all must learn how to exercise our spirit to minister Christ, apply Christ, and share Christ with others. This depends on our daily labor. If we do not labor on Christ and live by Christ, we will have nothing of Christ in our hand. Even if we understand how to exercise our spirit, we may have the technique but not the material. When we come to the meeting, our spirit may be positive, active, living, on the alert, and ready to exercise, but we may be poor and empty-handed, not having anything of Christ to minister. If this is so, we are worshipping in spirit but not in reality; we are in Jerusalem, but we do not have a surplus in our hands. Therefore, the church life depends on our daily exercise of the spirit and also on our daily walk in Christ. We have to labor on Christ, walk in Christ, live by Christ, and have many experiences of Christ. Then we will be rich in Christ and with Christ. When we come to the meeting, we will know how to exercise our spirit, and we will have much surplus of Christ.

CHAPTER TWO

OUR PRACTICE IN THE MEETINGS

Scripture Reading: John 4:24

In this chapter we shall consider some practical points concerning the meetings. Many seeking believers start to meet together, but after a certain time they disband and dissolve their meeting. Why does their meeting collapse? On the one hand, many believers are disgusted with any kind of organization. They say, "We do not like to have an organization. We have to come together in the spirit." However, they do not know how to come together in the spirit. They do not know how to exercise the spirit, how to exhibit Christ, and how to come together with the surplus of Christ. Eventually, they do not have an organization, but what they have is only emptiness. This causes their meeting to fall to pieces.

THE BASIC PRINCIPLE FOR
CHRISTIAN MEETINGS AND SERVICE

This is why we need to pay the price to exercise our spirit and labor on Christ day by day. I beg you to keep these matters in mind and put them into practice. The basic principle for Christian service is to exercise the spirit and to have Christ as our surplus to minister to others. Whether we pray, sing a hymn, give a testimony, give a message, speak in a certain tongue, or have an interpretation, it must be in the spirit with Christ as the surplus. We must learn how to exercise our spirit, and we must have the experiences of Christ. Then when we come together to meet, we will know the best and proper way to meet by exercising our spirit to exhibit Christ, ministering Christ by either a hymn, a prayer, a testimony, a message, or even a tongue. By any kind of manifestation of the Holy Spirit we must exercise our spirit to minister Christ to others. This is the proper way to have our meetings and service.

LABORING ON CHRIST
FOR AN EXHIBITION OF HIS RICHES

To improve any of the meetings requires three things. First we must labor on Christ. This is not a matter only of the meeting; it is a matter of our entire daily life. In these days the dear brothers and sisters truly have been helped and are practicing how to labor on Christ. This produces the riches for the meeting. In the ancient times the people of Israel came together three times a year—at the Passover, at Pentecost, and at the Feast of Tabernacles—with the surplus of the produce of the good land. This produce came from their day-by-day labor during that year. For the whole year they labored on the good land, so they had produce from the land as a rich surplus to bring for the Lord's worship. This rich surplus became an exhibition of the rich produce of the rich land. However, this depended on their daily labor on the good land.

The good land typifies Christ. Today Christ is the good land to us, so we must labor on Him. The rain, the sunshine, the air, and the fertile soil come from the grace of God, but we need to labor to till the ground, sow the seed, and take care of the harvest. This is to cooperate with God's grace. We need to pray and deal with many things. We need to learn how to trust in the Lord, abide in Him, fellowship with Him, and deal with Him and be dealt with by Him. This is a spiritual labor, not human struggling; it is not human effort but a spiritual coordination with the Lord.

Day by day we all must learn to live in this way. Then we will know Christ in a practical way and experience Him in our spirit, and when we come to the meetings, we will have something of Christ. We may be humble and say that we have nothing, but in actuality we will be full. We will have something, and spontaneously it will come out. This is why we all must learn how to live in Christ, walk by Christ, and experience Christ in the spirit. This is our constant labor on Christ. Then even if we do not give a testimony, we still will have the experience of Christ. When we simply open our mouth to praise and thank the Lord, we will be rich in our praise and thanks because we have something of Christ.

WORSHIPPING IN SPIRIT AND IN TRUTHFULNESS

Second, we need to exercise our spirit with the indwelling Holy Spirit to worship in spirit. When we exercise our spirit, the Holy Spirit cooperates and honors this. This is the true worship in spirit and in truthfulness (John 4:24). *Truthfulness* refers to reality, that is, to Christ who is reality. Today we worship God in spirit with Christ as the surplus that we bring to God as the reality.

BEING COORDINATED, STRONG, ACTIVE, AND POSITIVE

Third, we must learn how to cooperate and coordinate. The only way to worship is with Christ as our experience, with the spirit as our means, our instrument, and in coordination. If we have these three—Christ, the spirit, and coordination—the meetings will be wonderful and rich, full of Christ and living. They will be very good because we will have the riches, the spirit, and the way. We must pay our full attention to these three matters. Then whenever we come together, the meetings will be very attractive and attracting. They will attract people; people will be happy and anxious to come to the meetings. On the contrary, a meeting can be very low. Some brothers do seek the Lord and like to come to the meetings, but whenever they come to the meeting, they bring it lower; we need to be delivered from meeting in this way.

We all have to labor on Christ. We all have to learn how to exercise our spirit in the meeting to be active, not inactive, and positive, not negative. We should not sit and wait. That is not the time to wait; that is the time the Lord is waiting for us. We should exercise our spirit to be strong. Luke 1:80 says that John the Baptist grew and became strong in spirit. Whenever we come into the meetings we have to be strong in spirit and active and positive. Then we will not imprison the Holy Spirit within our spirit. The Holy Spirit will be released, and the release of the Holy Spirit will bring forth the riches of Christ. We all have to learn to release our spirit and exercise our spirit. Then we will be open. We will pave the way for the Holy Spirit within us to come out.

We must also learn the technique of how to coordinate. Once a brother starts in one way, we simply follow him. If his functioning is weak, we must learn to strengthen it, and if it is low, we must learn to uplift it. I look to the Lord that we will learn these practical things. We can be assured that if we put them into practice, the meetings of the church will be enriched, living, edifying, and very attractive. People will receive the real help, and the Lord will be glorified. The Lord's presence will be with us, and it will be easy to bring unbelievers to the Lord. This is our responsibility, and it has very much to do with the building up of the local church. A local church can be built up only through these practical matters. We all must put them into practice.

"PLAYING WITH THE SAME BALL" IN THE MEETINGS

A brother may begin a meeting by ministering something concerning Christ as patience. If we know how to exercise the spirit and if we have many experiences of Christ as the surplus in our hand, we can immediately follow the brother to give a testimony of how we experienced Christ as our patience. Or perhaps we will be ready to continue his ministering by offering a prayer to praise and thank the Lord that He is our patience. This may be compared to handling the same ball in a ball game. Sometimes, however, we may have only one item of the surplus of Christ. We may have nothing to say concerning Christ as patience, but we may have something to say about Christ as our strength. After the brother ministers Christ as patience, we do not have anything with which to follow him. Yet because we feel that we must exercise our spirit to do something, we start on another line. This is to play with a different "ball." After this, another brother may start another line; this is to play with yet another "ball." Eventually there will be many different lines in one meeting. That is like one team playing a game with many balls.

Sometimes a team of five members may play with more than five balls; one player plays with his ball, another plays with his, and another plays with a third ball. This is an illustration of a poor meeting. If we know how to discern, we can tell that many meetings are poor; we play with "ball" after "ball," not like a team but like naughty boys. Each one plays his own ball, and each one even has two or three balls. This is because we are not trained, educated, or exercised.

The Lord can testify for me that I have no intention to criticize anyone, but I must say that it is hard to find a Christian meeting that is truly satisfying. Many Christian meetings are always poor. There is always a dissatisfaction within the attendants. This is not our dissatisfaction only; it is the Lord's dissatisfaction. The Lord is not satisfied unless there is a proper meeting with a group of Christians who know how to exercise their spirit, have many experiences of Christ, and have the technique, the best way, the best exercise, to "play ball." The more we see this kind of meeting, the more we will be satisfied. We will not say, "This is a poor 'game.' I will never come back again to see this kind of 'game.'" This kind of meeting will attract people and edify them. I can testify that to be in such a meeting even once edifies people for their whole life. Such a meeting edifies and builds up.

COORDINATING TO CALL THE PROPER HYMNS

We may illustrate the way to begin a meeting with playing basketball. All basketball players know that they need a good start. If they start wrongly, they will lose the game; it is very hard to adjust a wrong start. At the start of a meeting, someone may call Hymn #127 in *Hymns,* that starts, "Hark! ten thousand voices crying." This hymn may be too high, so to adjust the meeting to a lower level, another brother may call Hymn #510, that begins, "I've found the One of peerless worth." These two hymns are two different "balls." One hymn is about the "air force," and the other is about the "marines"; after being "in the air," we immediately dive "under the sea." This is disgusting.

Hymn #127, written by J. N. Darby, is the highest of all hymns. We cannot find another hymn with such a high standard. Therefore, unless a meeting immediately starts in the third heaven, we should not use this hymn. Only once in my life, in 1943, have I been in a meeting that began in such a high way. I can never forget it. When the meeting started, it was very high. All of a sudden we began to sing, "Hark! ten thousand voices crying." Usually, however, we need to learn not to choose such a high hymn to start the meeting. If we start the meeting with such a high hymn, we will be frustrated; we will not know what to do next. This hymn is good for when the meeting has been going on and on. When the meeting comes to a climax, we can use this hymn; at that time it fits.

A brother may realize that a hymn is too high, so he may have the intention to adjust the meeting and have a new start. However, he may adjust the meeting from the "air" all the way down to the "sea." If we intend to adjust a hymn with too high a standard, we should not come down too quickly. We need to keep the meeting going in a proper way. After singing a hymn, the best way is to continue by reading, praising, and praying with paraphrases of the verses in order to digest the hymn.

To have a proper meeting is a matter of teamwork. A certain brother may know how to adjust the meeting, but he should not do too much. If he does, he will be the clergy, and the others will become the laity.

LEARNING TO COORDINATE WITH OTHERS

As we have seen, in a meeting we all need to learn to coordinate with others, like a team playing ball. We need to realize that we are on a team; we are not playing by ourselves. We should learn to follow others. We should always consider how the meeting has gone on; then we can simply continue on the same line. This is not always easy; it requires exercise and practice. If others are praising the Lord, we need to follow. This will protect us from practicing wrongly.

Some prayers are truly good, but they are given at the wrong time. We should not think that to have a good prayer means we are right. We may have a good prayer but offer it in a wrong way. At certain stages of a meeting we have to follow others to pray in certain ways. Again, this is like playing ball. We may play ball very well, but it may not be the right time to play in a certain way. We all have to learn this. We have had much improvement in our Lord's table meeting, but we still need to improve more. We still need to learn more and more.

OUR PRACTICE IN THE LORD'S TABLE MEETING

Serving Our "Dish" at the Right Time

In the Lord's table meeting, in the section for the remembrance of the Lord, a brother may offer a prayer of praise to the Father. We all realize that this is not fitting and needs to be adjusted.

Another brother may offer a prayer, saying, "Grant us Your blessing and anointing for the time to come." This prayer indicates that the time of worship is closed and it is now time for fellowship or other matters. After this prayer, however, three more persons may continue with worship. This indicates that the brother served "dessert" before the other "dishes" were finished; while dessert was being served, three more dishes came. On the one hand, it is good for the first brother to wait a little. On the other hand, however, the three brothers should not have hesitated; they should have served their dishes more quickly. If we do not serve our dish quickly before dessert comes, we had better forget our dish. If there is a hesitation, people will think that all the dishes have been served. We all must learn to do the right thing at the right time.

Offering Hymns and Prayers
That Fit the Feeling of the Meeting

Hymn #495 in *Hymns* says, "Christ is God's centrality / And His universality; / He is God's delight and joy / Throughout all eternity." This is a good hymn in itself, but the Lord's table is a weekly remembrance of the Lord. Therefore, all the hymns and prayers offered must keep the thought of the enjoyment of the Lord. A hymn on Christ as God's centrality and universality may be for our understanding and not for enjoyment, so it is better to use it for a message or testimony. If we read Hymn #495, we can see that there is no thought or sense of enjoyment, and without the sense of enjoyment we do not have the realization that we are remembering the

Lord. According to the understanding, it is good, but according to the sense, it does not fit the atmosphere of the Lord's table meeting. We have many good, spiritual hymns, but they do not fit the Lord's table meeting because they do not give the sense of the remembrance of the Lord.

After a while we will graduate from our study of the meetings, but after that we must go on to "graduate school" and even get a "Ph.D." We must continue to learn.

CHAPTER THREE

BEING RELATED
AND TAKING CARE OF OTHERS

Scripture Reading: Eph. 4:16; S. S. 1:7-8; Matt. 4:18-22; John 4:24

ALL FUNCTIONING TO MINISTER IN THE MEETINGS

As we said in the first chapter, we do not use the word *service* in the way today's Christianity uses it. We refer to the Christian service as having several main items. First it is the function of ministering in the meetings. This means that every believer must function, that is, minister, in the meetings.

The so-called message meeting, the meeting for giving a message, is not as important as the other meetings. The meetings such as the Lord's table meeting, the prayer meeting, the fellowship meeting, and the study meeting are all much more important than the message meeting. In today's Christianity, however, people mostly pay attention to the meetings for preaching, teaching, and ministry, so they have a minister or a preacher to preach and to teach, while everyone else sits in the pews to listen. This is not what the believers did at the beginning of the church age. Rather, this is something degraded. We should not bring this to the church life. It is part of the leaven mentioned in Matthew 13:33, and we have to drop it. The church service must include meetings for believers to come together to function mutually. In the Lord's table meeting we all have to learn how to exercise our spirit to minister to others and to function, and in the prayer meeting, the fellowship meeting, and the study meeting it is the same. When we come together, we all need to learn to function one with another. This is the first item in the Christian service.

BEING RELATED TO ONE ANOTHER

The second item in the Christian service is that we need to learn to be related one to another. In order to minister as functioning members, we have to learn to be related to others. Consider the members of your body. All the different members must be rightly related one to another. If the arm is not related to other members, it cannot function properly; before an arm can function, it must be related rightly with the other members. When we offer a prayer, give a testimony, or minister in another way in a meeting, it seems that there is no need to be related with others. However, in order to serve the Lord, to be a living member in the Body, we must realize that we need relatedness. We need to be related with others. Before we are going to serve or do anything as living members of the Body, we first must be related with others.

Being Related in a Definite Way to Several Others

What is the way to be related with others? Again, consider your body. Every member is related to one, two, or three other members. The arm, for example, is related on one end to the shoulder and on the other end to the hand. We can say that we are members in the Body, but we must know what members we are directly and definitely related to. If we ask an arm, it will tell us definitely that it is related to the shoulder and to the hand. We should not say merely in a general way, "I am in the church; I am a member in the Body." We must know to whom we are related.

In a building, every piece of material is related to other pieces. A stone that is built into a building is directly related to at least four or five other stones. On the right there is one piece, on the left there is another piece, on the top is another, and beneath is another. In order to be built up in the church, we need to have some brothers and sisters directly related to us. We cannot be in the Body in a general way.

It is not good enough to be related to only one or two others, because these one or two may merely be our favorites.

We may like a certain brother, so day by day we try to be related to him. We must be related to several others; then we will be balanced. At our right hand we need one brother, at our left hand we need another one, in front we need another, behind we need another, and on top we need still another. We need at least five or six to balance us. To be sure, if we can go on with these five or six, we can go on with the whole Body. But if we cannot go on with these five or six, I am assured we will not go on with the Body.

Being Balanced, Adjusted, and Corrected by Our Relatedness

Some brothers and sisters are very clever. They are transcendent, like the birds in the air. They do not like to be related to anyone. To some extent they are "supernatural," not real and practical. They are in the church, but they are related to no one. This is because they are afraid to be balanced, adjusted, and corrected. In order to be balanced rightly and adequately, we need at least six brothers or sisters to balance us. We may say that we are related to a certain brother, but he is only one. We need a second, third, fourth, fifth, and sixth one. Try this. To have six brothers or six sisters in the church to be related with means that we are fully balanced.

Whatever we are going to do, we should fellowship with these six persons. If any one of the six would not agree with us, we should forget about what we are doing. Then we will see how much we will be balanced. Many people say they are seeking the Lord's leading, but to have six brothers or six sisters to balance us is the best leading of the Lord. Some brothers may even need twelve others. If certain ones have twelve others to balance them, they will have much improvement after only two months. If the twelve say it is right to do something, we should do it, but if even one of the twelve feels we should do something else, then we should do that instead. This is the guidance from the Lord. I am not speaking this lightly. If an arm does something, it has to have the agreement of the shoulder and the hand. If either of these two members says, "No, I do not agree," the arm cannot move. This is not merely a teaching; it is something very practical.

Being Related to Particular Ones
for Support and Protection

If we cannot say to whom we are related, this means we are not yet built into the Body. If we are material built into the building, we are able to point to the other materials above us, beneath us, to the left and right of us, and in front and in back of us. If you ask me to whom I am related, I will tell you that I am related to many persons. If even one of these brothers says, "Brother Lee, we do not feel this matter is right," I will not do it. It seems that this is our limitation, but it is not a limitation; it is a support. The more we are related to our fellow members, the more we are supported and protected by them. Consider the pieces of the material in a building. Every piece is supported and protected by many other pieces. Why are some persons so weak? It is because they are isolated. An entire building, however, can stand against the strong wind and the heavy rain, against the blowing of the strongest storm. This is because all the pieces are built together, supporting one another and protecting one another.

Before we go on to see other items related to the service, we must stress this point very much. If we are not related to anyone else, it will be impossible for us to serve properly. All the items of the Christian service which we will speak of depend on this relatedness. When I was young, I did not know this secret. I tried to overcome many things, but I did not succeed. One day I came to know the secret that I need to be related to my fellow members, and by the mercy of the Lord, I did become related. After I became related to the members, it was very easy to overcome things. If we have a weakness, a weak point which is hard to overcome, we should not try to overcome it by ourselves. We simply should be related to some brothers and sisters and bring that weak point to them. Then we will overcome it immediately and spontaneously.

The Need to Help the Believers to Be Related

As we have said, some brothers need to have at least four or six brothers related with them, while other brothers need ten, twelve, or even more. The more we are related to others, the more strength we have, the more victory we have, and the more protection we have. No one can arrange some brothers or sisters for us to be related with; we need to go to the Lord and seek His guidance for this. However, for the church to be built up, the responsible brothers, the leading ones, should help the brothers and sisters to be related to others. If the leading ones have the time, they should take care of all the brothers and sisters one by one. Two or three leading brothers can spend time with a brother to fellowship with him, saying, "Brother, what do you feel? To whom should you be related?" After a short time, they can help another brother to be related, and after a few days they can help a certain sister to be related. They should help the building materials to be built up with others. Human arrangement does not work, but this kind of help truly works. This is why we need the leading ones, both brothers and sisters, who know how to be related with others and how to help others to be related, not merely by arranging but by spiritual fellowship. In this way all the brothers and sisters will be related one to another.

If we are related to certain brothers, and each of these brothers is related to others, we will be like a chain that is interwoven and intertwined. In this way there is the real building of the Body, not as an organization but as something related in life and in the Spirit. Nothing can damage this building, and nothing can break this kind of relatedness. This is the Body. We speak much about the Body; we say that all Christians are members of the Body. However, where is the Body today? We have the many members, but we may not have the Body. Merely to have the many members is not to have the Body. In order to have the Body, all the members must be livingly related.

In the same way, merely to have a heap of materials is not to have the building. That is not the building; it is a heap. The materials have been heaped up but not yet built up. Are we heaped up, or are we built up? I have seen many Christians meeting together, but I am sorry to say that they are only heaped up. Sometimes they are not even heaped up in a good order. They are heaped upside down, fighting, quarrelling, and debating all the time. This is not the building. The building is the members being rightly related. The proper phrase used by the Scriptures is *joined together* (Eph. 4:16). We need to be joined together with others in a practical way, not merely in doctrine.

We need to pray much for this purpose in particular. So that the Lord can build us up together, we must be definitely related with at least four, five, six, ten, or twelve brothers and sisters. Whatever we do in our home life, private life, school life, or business life, we need to fellowship with these brothers and sisters to whom we are related. This is a safeguard, protection, strengthening, and real support. Unless the brothers and sisters are built up in this way, there is no possibility that a local church can be built up. We may have meeting after meeting, but we are not being built up together until we are related with one another in a definite way, until every one of us can point to some and say, "I am related to these brothers." This is a real mutual help for one another. Again I say, we are not merely presenting teachings and messages; we are pointing out the way for us to serve the Lord.

Being Related according to the Lord's Sovereignty

We should ask, "Lord, to whom should I be related?" Before we start to minister, to serve, to do our duty as living members, we need to solve the problem of being related with others. We all have to check ourselves with this matter. Then we will see what kind of help we will receive simply by being related to many dear ones.

We must learn to be related to persons who are not of our choosing according to our taste. If we have the choice to be related according to our taste, we eventually will be related to no one but ourselves. We will take ourselves as our best choice. We must learn to sacrifice, to crucify, our taste and to submit to others. If the Lord sovereignly brings together a number of brothers, they need to submit one to another. No one should say, "I don't like to be with these brothers. I will join myself to someone else." This does not work. We need to believe the Lord is sovereign and learn to submit ourselves under His sovereignty.

I believe in the Lord's sovereignty. As a person from the Far East, I could never be here without the Lord's sovereignty. Even five or six years ago I could not have dreamed that I would be in the United States. I do not know where I will be next year; the Lord is sovereign concerning this. But at this time His sovereignty has put me here, so I have to submit myself to the brothers here. I should not say, "The brothers in the Far East are wonderful." I should not appreciate the brothers in the Far East in this way. Rather, I have to appreciate the brothers who are with me by the Lord's sovereignty. We must learn to take His sovereignty. Whoever lives in a certain place should submit himself to the brothers in his place. He should not say that he likes the brothers in another place. We have to learn this lesson. In this matter, we need to be broken and to be built. This is a real test.

TAKING CARE OF OTHERS

After we are related, there is still one thing that is very important: We must take care of others. To be related to others is one thing, but to take care of others is another thing. This is the real outreach. This outreach includes gospel preaching, outreach to the unbelievers. It also includes visitation, fellowship, with younger believers. Before we go to take care of others, we first need to be related with others. To be related with others is to get the help from others. Then when we get the help, we are able to help others. We all must learn to take care of these two aspects, the aspect of being related to brothers and sisters to receive the help, to be strengthened, supported, protected, and guarded, and the aspect of taking care of others. This is the proper service, function, and activity of Christians.

The Need to Be Balanced and without Extremes

We need to work to take care of, to reach, these two kinds of people, the unbelievers and the believers. With nearly every matter, people in Christianity today have gone to extremes, some to one extreme, and some to the other. Even in preaching the gospel, in the outreach, Christians are on two extremes. Many Christians are on the extreme of acting too much. Others are the co-called or self-named spiritual persons who do not like to act without the Lord's guidance. To wait and not act without the Lord's guidance in this way is something human, soulish, and natural; it is not something of the Lord. I see this today, as I have seen this many times in the past. These so-called, self-named spiritual persons have been waiting for years, but they never have the guidance from the Lord. It seems they are waiting on a Lord who never acts. They say, "Without the Lord's guidance, I would not move," but they have been waiting for years, and still there is no guidance. This is an extreme. We need to be balanced, not being on one extreme or the other.

The way to be balanced is first to have fellowship with the Lord, second to have fellowship with the brothers to whom we are related, and then to take some action. We need to say, "Lord, I know that after I have been placed and built into the Body, I must be a member in fellowship and a member in function. I know that my duty, my responsibility, is to take care of the unbelievers and believers."

Contacting Unbelievers
to Have a One-fold Increase Yearly

We need to take care of the unbelievers. When the Lord comes back, He will ask us about the unbelievers. We cannot tell the Lord, "I did not have guidance from You." The Lord has given us the guidance already. At least we have our relatives, neighbors, friends, classmates, and many persons on the street. It is one hundred percent right that every Christian has to have some part in gospel preaching. This is our duty. Why do we not do it? There are many reasons why, but one of the most important reasons is that we are not rightly related to the other brothers and sisters. If we are rightly related to our fellow members, we will have some work of gospel preaching.

To have the outreach is one hundred percent right, but we should not make it a regulation. Still, it is right to encourage the brothers and sisters to bring at least one person to the

Lord yearly. It sounds like a small thing to bring one person to the Lord in three hundred and sixty-five days. However, if we now have one hundred people meeting together, and each one brings one yearly, the next year we will have two hundred people, one-fold increase. Then the third year we will have four hundred, the fourth year eight hundred, the fifth year sixteen hundred, the sixth year thirty-two hundred, the seventh year sixty-four hundred, and the eighth year twelve thousand eight hundred. This is marvelous. I do not say this to push you; I simply say that this is our duty.

Having Effectual Contact with People by Our Relatedness

Why would we not fulfill this duty? It is because we are not rightly related. If the saints are willing to be built up, our number will increase more than one-fold yearly. In 1949 in Taipei, the capital of Taiwan, we had close to a thirty-fold increase in only a year, from about thirty to fifty people to over one thousand. This was possible because of our related-ness. With relatedness we are very prevailing to bring people to the Lord. We may have a relative who is not saved, and it may be hard for us to help him to be saved. However, if we are related to the brothers or sisters, we can ask all those to whom we are related to help us. For one or two nights we can invite our relative and all these dear brothers to our home. Perhaps twelve persons can be there, giving testimony after testimony with much convincing speaking. In this way others can help us to convince our relative, and then we with the others will help to convince his neighbor. This is the way the brothers in Taipei did their preaching. They did not trust in preaching in public places. Of course, they had much preach-ing in public, but they did not trust only in that.

To preach in the way of inviting someone to come to our home for dinner is more practical than public preaching. When they come, there will be twelve persons waiting for them. How can they resist? This is what it means to be related. We do not preach the gospel or deal with our relatives by ourselves. We are the members related to the whole Body. Sometimes after the Lord's table, a brother in Taipei would stand to say that he had a neighbor who needed to be saved. This person may have been a worshipper of Buddha, so the brother would ask the whole church to pray for him. Because the whole church prayed, it was easy to deal with the Buddhist. There is no need to go into detail about how to do this. I have just given some hints that we must put into practice. If we are first related to others and then go to serve, work, and preach, we will see the results.

The Real, Practical, and Prevailing Way to Preach the Gospel

We should first put the names of all the persons we know—our relatives, neighbors, classmates, and friends—on a list and check one by one whether each one has been saved. Then we should consider each name and seek the Lord's guidance. The Lord will be with us and will burden us with at least two or three persons for the present time. Then we must pray for them and seek the Lord's guidance as to how to contact them. The Lord may lead us to send them some books or tracts or to have some kind of contact with them. In this way we will have the wisdom and power to move and work. In addition, we should refer these matters to the brothers and sisters to whom we are related. This will be a real, practical, and prevailing preaching of the gospel, and it will be very fruitful. After a certain time, of course, the church may have a gospel preaching meeting. Then we should bring our friends or the persons for whom we are concerned. It will be easy for them to be saved.

We have to encourage one another to bring at least one unbeliever to the Lord yearly. As a local church we have to produce something for the Lord. We should not be on one extreme nor on the other extreme. We need to be in the middle to be balanced. We know how to fellowship with the Lord, and we know how to fellowship with the saints and to be built up in the Body. Then we function to produce something for the Lord. I am one hundred percent sure that we will see that this is truly effective and prevailing. We will see people saved through us, and not only once a year. The Holy Spirit will honor this, and this will stir up our spirit. The more we love others, the more we love sinners for the Lord's sake, the more we will be strong in the spirit.

Bearing the Responsibility
to Contact New Ones after a Meeting

When we come to the meetings, we all have to learn to take care of others. We must learn to take care not only of unbelievers but also of the believers, the younger ones. There are at least certain ones younger than we are. We should try our best to help them. This is the best way to open ourselves. Many times it is not easy for us to be open with others. Recently, for example, we had a large attendance in the Lord's table meeting. There were a good number of new ones, so I exercised myself to watch the situation. Regrettably, not many brothers and sisters took care of them. Each person went to be with someone familiar, but no one took care of the new ones. There is something wrong with this. If some new ones attend a meeting, immediately after the meeting our responsibility is to take care of them. We all have to learn this. We must not think that this is the responsibility of the leading ones. In this sense everyone among us is a leading brother or leading sister; we all have to take the lead. In this way we will be exercised to be enlarged. We will be open to others, and our capacity will be enlarged.

In Song of Songs 1:7 the seeking one asks the Lord, "Tell me, you whom my soul loves, / Where do you pasture your flock? / Where do you make it lie down at noon? / For why should I be like one who is veiled / Beside the flocks of your companions?" The Lord answers, "If you yourself do not know, / You fairest among women, / Go forth on the footsteps of the flock, / And pasture your young goats / By the shepherds' tents" (v. 8). The seeker is telling the Lord that she needs His feeding and rest, and she wants to know where she can find it. The Lord answers that she must follow the steps of the flock, the church. However, this is not the whole answer. She must also pasture her young goats by the shepherds' tents. The seeking one is taking care of herself, but the Lord's answer is to remind her to take care of her young ones.

Casting the Nets and Mending the Nets

At the start of the Lord's ministry, the Lord called two pairs of disciples (Matt. 4:18-22). The first pair was Peter and Andrew his brother, and the second pair was James and John his brother. These were the first four disciples called by the Lord. When Peter and Andrew were called, they were casting a net into the sea to catch fish, so the Lord told them, "I will make you fishers of men." When the Lord called the second pair, John and James, they were mending their nets. Casting a net and mending the nets are the two main aspects of the Lord's ministry. In the service of contacting people the first aspect is to cast the net, and the second aspect is to mend the net. What does it mean to cast the net? This is to be the fishers of men, to bring people in. What then is it to mend the net? This is to bring people back to the beginning. The apostle John was the last of the writers of the books of the New Testament, and his writings always brought people back to the beginning. When the church drifted away, John tried his best to bring the church back. This was the real mending.

In the church there is the need of the ministry in the first aspect, to cast the net, to bring people in. Then after people are brought in, they need to be kept and protected, so there is the need of the mending. It is very interesting that at the beginning of the Lord's ministry He called these two kinds of disciples to follow Him. We have to follow the Lord and serve Him as disciples casting the net and mending the net, that is, bringing others in and always keeping people in. On the one hand, we need to deal with the unbelievers as fishers casting the net, and on the other hand, we need to deal with the younger believers as the "young goats" (S. S. 1:8).

We often pray, "Lord, bring the seeking ones together." We are not only the seeking ones; we are the seeking ones seeking for the seeking ones. However, we should ask ourselves who we are related to, how many unbelievers we are bringing to the Lord, and how many "young goats," younger believers, we have. If we check in this way, we will be exposed as to where we are and what we are. It is not right for a group of believers to have meeting after meeting, but after one or two years their number still remains the same. There is something wrong with this, and there is no excuse for this. We should not say that in America it is different from Taiwan. Rather, we must learn how to serve the Lord to carry out both kinds of outreach after we are related to others: caring for the unbelievers and caring for the younger believers. If we do, then every younger one in the church will have some brothers or sisters to take care of him or her. This will help the church life, and many problems will be solved by this care. I beg you to bring these matters to the Lord. This is not a mere teaching; rather, we need to put all these things into practice.

We must learn to be related with others; then we will have strength, power, and even authority. Then we must start to take care of the unbelievers. There are many people in Los Angeles, for example; perhaps over a million people here are not saved. It is a sea full of different kinds of fish. How can we not touch any fish in such a big sea? We have to learn how to bring people to the Lord. Then we must learn how to take care of at least one or two younger ones in the church as our spiritual "young goats." In this way these "young goats" will be our nourishment. The more we take care of them, the more we will be nourished, and the more we will grow.

I do look to the Lord that we all may be brought to the realization that, by the mercy of the Lord, we must be related with others, begin to reach the unbelievers to bring them to the Lord, and reach the younger Christians to take care of them. Although these practical matters are often not practiced in today's Christianity, I beg you to put them into practice. Then you will see that the Lord will honor you and the Holy Spirit will go along with you. You will have the position, the ground, the standing, to claim the riches of Christ and the power of the Holy Spirit.

CHAPTER FOUR

LABORING WITH DIFFERENT CATEGORIES OF PEOPLE

Scripture Reading: Acts 2:47

BEARING OUR DAILY RESPONSIBILITY TO BRING PEOPLE TO THE LORD

In a normal condition, a local church must always increase not only in life but also in numbers. Acts 2:47 says of the church in Jerusalem, "And the Lord added together day by day those who were being saved." The new converts added to the church were brought in by the laboring saints. We often have the wrong concept that people are brought into the church through a gospel campaign or a certain kind of gospel activity. According to the first few chapters of Acts, however, many new converts were continually brought into the church, not through this kind of gospel preaching and ministry but through the labor of the believers. For this reason, we stress that every member of the Body has the function, duty, and responsibility to bring people to the Lord.

To bring people to the Lord is not a hard task. Rather, it is a daily labor, a responsibility which we must bear in a daily way. We should write down a list of the names of all the people we know. Then we should consider these names and pray for them. While we are doing this, the Lord will anoint us concerning certain names. We will have a realization that we must take care of a certain two or three at the present time. Then we should pray for these two or three specifically by name and fellowship with the Lord about the way to contact them and that the Lord would give us the best approach. Then we will know what we have to do, whether it is to write them, send them booklets or testimonies, or visit them. The Lord will give the guidance.

OUR NEED FOR TRAINING
AND THE PROPER TECHNIQUE

The foregoing is the principle of bringing people to the Lord, but we still need the details. In doing anything, we need the right technique. Even if we have the heart to do something, if we do not have the technique, it is hard to do it in a good way. Therefore, we must learn the technique. Of course, we know that we must pray much, trust in the Lord, and claim His power; there is no need to speak much about this. Even if we pray much and have power, however, we still need the technique. Many times the technique paves the way for the Lord to move; it is a good cooperation with the power from on high.

If we read the record of Acts, we can see that Peter was a trained person. He had been with the Lord for three and a half years; when the Lord was on the earth, He purposed and intended to train Peter. Although Peter was a fisherman, it is wrong to think that he did not know much. When we read how Peter stood on the day of Pentecost, ministered a message, and handled the situation, we can realize that he was a person who was fully trained. He had not only the power from on high and the anointing but also the technique.

We should not think that even if we know nothing one day, overnight we will receive power from on high to be more wonderful than an angel. This is a dream. If this were the case, there would have been no need for the disciples' training for the three and a half years prior to that day of Pentecost. Even after the Lord resurrected, He spent forty days with the disciples before His ascension, perhaps mostly to train Peter. By the day of Pentecost, Peter was one who was trained. Consider the way he spoke and handled the situation. He was full of training. We need this kind of training.

The Principle of Incarnation
Being the Cooperation of Man with God

We may have a heart and desire concerning a certain person,

and we may pray much for him and claim the Lord's power, but when we are with him, what will we do? We may look to the Lord for His guidance, but without training and technique, it is hard for the Lord to guide us. Many Christians today miss the mark. They say that we can do nothing because we are only human. It is true that we are human and that we can do nothing, but we must depend on the Lord and trust in Him. In the New Testament dispensation, the service of the Lord is in the principle of incarnation, which is the mingling of God with man and the cooperation of man with God.

God needs our cooperation. If there is no one raised up and trained by the Lord to be used by Him, the Lord cannot move. Again consider the book of Acts. The Lord could provide an angel to tell Cornelius to send for someone, but He could not and would not send an angel to preach the gospel to him (Acts 10:1-7, 34-43). The Lord needed a Peter who was trained to cooperate with Him. Without Peter's cooperation the gospel could not have been preached to the Gentile Cornelius.

Today it is the same with us. Almost two thousand years ago the Lord said that the gospel must be preached to the uttermost part of the earth (1:8). The Lord has been ready, but why have almost two thousand years passed and the gospel has still not been preached to the uttermost parts? This is not due to the Lord; it is due to us. The cooperation on the part of man has not been adequate. We may be small in number, but if we are ready and trained and if we go along with the Lord, after only three months our number will be not only doubled but tripled. Some may say that I am following the evangelizing denominations to push people to preach the gospel, but I am not forcing or pushing anyone. I am only saying that the Lord is waiting for us. He is ready, but He is waiting for us to be ready. If we are ready, we will see the results. This is why we feel the need for training.

Our Cooperation Bringing In
the Lord's Anointing with His Presence

Recently the meeting for the Lord's table among us has very much improved. Is this because the brothers and sisters love the Lord more than they did a few months ago or they have more ability and stature of spirituality? No, it is due mostly to our learning and training. The brothers and sisters to some degree have learned the technique for the Lord's table meeting. Along with the improvement there has been the anointing with the Lord's presence. In the past we did not have the anointing with the Lord's presence as much as we now do because we did not have much training and cooperation to meet the Lord's need. The more cooperation we afford the Lord, the more He grants us His anointing with His presence. The more we are ready, the more the Lord will do through us. Therefore in the matter of bringing people to the Lord, we need the technique and training.

FIVE MAIN CATEGORIES OF PERSONS

After we have the burden for someone, pray for him, and receive the anointing and the power from on high, what shall we do with him? In order to deal with a person, we must know how to categorize or classify him, just like a fisherman knows the categories of fish. If a fisherman classifies his fish, he will know what kind of bait to use. A certain bait may be good for one kind of fish, but to use the wrong bait will scare the fish away. If we classify people, we will know what they need.

To properly classify people, we must have the right technique. We would not be so foolish as to ask someone what kind of person he is. Rather, we can classify people by contacting them in a general way through conversation. We should be general and not make a display to them that we are religious, spiritual, or heavenly. People do not like to talk to angels or religious persons; this scares them. Rather, we must talk to people in a general, human way. Then by our general talk, we must learn to realize what kind of person each one is.

In the past I have given more than twenty classifications of people, but here it is sufficient to give only five main categories. The first is a so-called atheist, someone who does not believe that there is a God in the universe. It is easy to find out if a person is an atheist. The second category is people who are sinful and living in sins. These also are easy to know. The third classification is people who sense the vanity of this life. They always have the sense that life is vain, a vanity of vanities. The fourth classification is moral people, people who always pay attention to morality. The last classification includes professing Christians. If we know these classifications, it is easy to realize what category a person belongs to. Then we will know how to deal with him.

Dealing with Atheists

In principle, the best way to contact an atheist for the gospel is never to argue. Rather, we must touch his feeling. Atheists are strong in their mentality, but regardless of how strong people are in their mind, they have a certain amount of feeling concerning God. In their mind there is no God, and in their mouth there is no God, but in their heart there is a feeling. We should realize that many times when an atheist is saying there is no God, an inner voice within him is saying, "Suppose there is a God. What would you do?" There is an inner voice and an inner feeling. Therefore, we must learn not to argue with their mentality but strike their feeling in a nice way.

After touching their feeling, we should touch their conscience. Even atheists have a conscience, and in their conscience there is the consciousness that they are wrong in certain things. This is the ground for us to take to speak something that they may be convinced not from without but from within. A person is a human, not a lower animal like a bird or the cattle. Within man in God's creation there are certain things according to God's nature. Even if we do not have the words to express or explain it, we realize that within our human nature there is something that senses there is a God. We cannot explain this, but we sense it. A young man may be able to boldly say that there is no God, but the older he becomes, the more weakly he will say this. When he comes to the verge of death, he will have no more boldness to say there is no God. This is because the inner sense created by God within our nature becomes stronger and stronger as we grow older. The older we become, the stronger this inner sense is. There is no argument against this.

Someone may say to us that he still does not believe. However, we can tell him that within him is something that believes. This may cause him to not sleep for the whole night. In this way we pave the way for the Holy Spirit to work in him. Sometimes a strong person can say that for many years he was not convinced, but this inner voice was always speaking. Eventually, such a person will be convinced. There is no need to argue. Rather, we should learn to touch people's feeling and conscience. This is the principle of speaking with an atheist. If we practice this, we will see that it works.

Dealing with Sinners

There are two kinds of people who live in sins. The first has no consciousness of sin. They are very careless and do not care that they are living in sins. The best way to deal with them is not to condemn but to point out the damage, pains, and consequences of sins. We can illustrate this to them with a real situation, showing them that the more they sin, the more damage they will suffer and the quicker they will die. Neither a gambler, a smoker, or a drinker can have a long life. Then we can bring them to the realization that after death there will still be a further consequence. Death is not the end of the consequences of sin. However, we should not talk too much about the future judgment; it is better to talk about the present life. In this way we will create the consciousness of sin within them.

The second kind of persons who live in sins is those who live in sins with the consciousness that they are sinful but do not have the strength to save themselves. They are convicted, but they do not know how to be saved and delivered. If we know how, it is very easy to help this kind of person. We simply point out to them that deliverance is not in ourselves but in Christ. In order to enjoy and partake of deliverance, we need to receive the redemption of Christ. Only Christ can deliver us from the bondage of sin; only Christ can free us. A person must realize that he is sinful and that Christ died for him on the cross. He needs to receive this redemption and stand on the ground of redemption; then he can claim and enjoy the deliverance of Christ. This is the principle of dealing with this kind of person.

Dealing with People Who Sense the Vanity of Life

It is also easy to help people who sense the vanity of life. The principle in dealing with this kind of person is to point out the reason for the sense of vanity. It is because the real fullness of human life is God Himself. From the very beginning man was made an empty vessel to contain God. As a container we need the content, and God is the content for man. If one does not have God, he is empty. This is the reason that people have the sense of vanity in their lives. God is the fullness, satisfaction, and very meaning of human life. To give a person this kind of instruction is effective. This is the principle, but how to use and develop it depends on us.

Dealing with Moral People

The fourth category of people is the moral people. Some brothers tell people that human morality does not matter, but a moral person will argue with this. It is foolish to tell unbelievers that morality does not mean anything. It is not easy to convince even a Christian that mere human morality means nothing. The best way is to admit that we need morality, but that morality is like the fruit of a tree; it comes out of a certain life. If we have this life, we have this kind of fruit, but if we do not have this life, how can we have the fruit? We may have some kind of fruit, but it is poor fruit. We admire that many people do have morality, but one must admit that this morality is not up to the highest standard because people do not have the life that is up to the highest standard. By speaking in this way we can point out that Christ is the highest life. If someone receives Christ, He will be his highest life, and he will bear the highest and best fruit. In this way, we can create in such a person a desire for the Lord. This is the principle of dealing with moral people, but we must learn how to use this principle in a very living and flexible way.

Dealing with Professing Christians

The fifth category of people is professing Christians. A

professing Christian is a Christian in name who does not know if he is saved. In principle, we must find the way to help this kind of person to realize that he is saved, to have the assurance of God's salvation. We should read some verses from the Scriptures to prove what a real believer is and to prove that a believer should have the assurance of salvation, knowing that his sins are forgiven and that Christ is his life. The principle is to help professing Christians to be clear about salvation.

USING THE SCRIPTURES TO DEAL WITH DIFFERENT KINDS OF PERSONS

We need to use the verses of the Scriptures when dealing with the above kinds of people. Here I will point out only a few; you must spend time to find the best verses.

Someone may say that the best verse to use to touch the feeling of an atheist is Psalm 14:1, which says, "The fool has said in his heart, / There is no God." However this offends people; this is to call them a fool. Rather, we may use Romans 1:19-20, which says, "Because that which is known of God is manifest within them, for God manifested it to them. For the invisible things of Him, both His eternal power and divine characteristics, have been clearly seen since the creation of the world, being perceived by the things made, so that they would be without excuse." If we use this verse, the feeling of an atheist will be touched.

For people who live in sins without the consciousness of sin, the best word is Romans 6:23, which says, "For the wages of sin is death." We should read this verse to this kind of person. There are many verses from the Scriptures that tell us the pain, damage, and loss caused by a life in sin. For those who live in sins with the consciousness of sin but without the strength to save themselves, we should show them verses that tell us that Christ died for our sins, such as 1 Peter 2:24 and 2 Corinthians 5:21. This kind of verses mostly deals with redemption. Then after this, we can give them some verses that confirm the deliverance of the living Lord, such as John 8:34 and 36, which tell us that the Lord as the Son of God is able to set us free from the bondage of sin.

For a person who senses the vanity of life, we can use Ephesians 2:12, which says, "Having no hope and without God in the world." If one does not have God, he has no hope. We may also use John 4:13 and 14, which say, "Jesus answered and said to her, Everyone who drinks of this water shall thirst again, but whoever drinks of the water that I will give him shall by no means thirst forever; but the water that I will give him will become in him a fountain of water gushing up into eternal life." In principle, we need to find the proper passages for each kind of person.

We especially need the Scriptures to deal with professing Christians. In principle, we should always use 1 John 5:13, which says, "I have written these things to you that you may know that you have eternal life, to you who believe into the name of the Son of God." God has written "these things." By His written word we have the proof, the testimony, that we have eternal life, forgiveness of sins, redemption, justification, and the Lord's salvation. We need to find the proper passages to convince people, not by our reasonings or arguments, but by the written word.

We need to learn passages such as the foregoing ones. Then when we contact people, we will know how to handle them. If we practice this, we will pave the way for the work of the Holy Spirit. A farmer knows how to till the ground, sow the seed, and water it. This paves the way for the life within the seed to grow. The life is in the seed, but there is the need for the cooperation of the farmer; that is, there is the need for a technique. If the technique is realized, the life within the seed will have a way to spring up and express itself. If we know the principle of how to handle different situations, a seed will be sown into people's hearts, and the Holy Spirit will work in them.

OPENING OUR HOMES
BEING THE BEST WAY TO HELP PEOPLE

We should not wait ten years to put these principles into practice. We need to practice them right away. From now on we all must go to the Lord, pray, and seek His guidance as to whom we should care for. The best way to help people is to open our homes and invite them in. It is especially easy to help students in this way. We should invite one or two, not too many. If we feel the need, we can invite another one or two brothers to help us. We should practice this over the long run, weekly or biweekly, and not expect a fast success.

LABORING DAILY TO BEAR ONE FRUIT YEARLY

If we all practice this for the long run, people will be brought into the church; every month we will bring forth new fruit. Each month ten or twenty people may be brought in through all the living and functioning members. Some may labor for half a year and still have no fruit, but they still must go on and labor. Perhaps after twelve months of labor they will bear fruit. Over the long run we will have fruit. If each one bears one fruit yearly, our number will double each year. This is a good result. If we labor as a daily duty, it should be easy to bring one person in twelve months. Do not expect to have a fast result. Rather, we must do our duty and labor with patience.

I was raised in Christianity, but when I was sixteen or seventeen years old, I rebelled and gave up Christianity. Then my second sister, who is older than I, was saved, and she asked a pastor, a true brother in the Lord, to help me. That pastor came to me once a week for several months. Every week he came just to sit with me. He did not say much; he only said, "Please come to our church next Sunday. Will you come?" I was not in the habit of doing that, so I did not go, but the next week he would come again and do the same thing. Perhaps once in eight or ten visits he would say a little about God's mercy or something else. He did this every week for almost half a year. Then the Chinese New Year came. According to the Chinese custom, people have many things to do at the close of the year, so the pastor said, "I realize you have many things to do, so for a few weeks you must excuse me for not coming." In my heart I said, "It is good that you will not come." During this time, of course, my sister must have prayed much for me.

The second day of the new year, according to custom, is the best day for New Year festivities. On that day when I rose from breakfast, my mother asked me where I would go. I could not answer. I said, "Where should I go? Perhaps I should go to the church." My mother was happy and encouraged me to go. That was the first time I came back to Christianity. Although I was not saved at that time, that was the start of the work of the Holy Spirit in me. This happened through the labor of that pastor. This shows us that we have to labor. It may seem that there is no result for a long time, but sooner or later something will come out if we sow the seed and labor on people.

There are many different aspects to a proper church life, and one aspect is that we must bring people to the Lord. We should not neglect this aspect. We must be balanced. We cannot meet week after week, month after month, and year after year, yet bring no new ones into the church. This is wrong. We should be adjusted in this matter. Even if we are young and weak, we still have to do something to bring people in; then we will be balanced and strengthened. If in a few months ten or twenty are baptized and added to the church, we all will be strengthened by the addition of these new converts. Therefore, we must all encourage one another concerning this matter.

LABORING IN A NORMAL WAY FOR THE LONG RUN

I beg you to have an outreach and take care of unbelievers. We must immediately put this into practice, and we must encourage one another. The brothers often invite the ones they are familiar with to come together. I always shake my head when I hear of this mutual inviting. They should not mutually invite each other so many times; rather, they should invite new ones. Sometimes we may even invite people off the street to eat dinner with us. Some have been saved in this way.

We must take care of unbelievers for the Lord's sake. Sometimes we say that we do not have time to invite unbelievers, but we seem to have time to invite the ones familiar to us. We should invite some new ones and younger ones. If someone comes to our meeting, we can invite him for fellowship. Then we will see a result. We should not dream; we should labor in a normal way day by day.

In Shanghai in the 1930s there was an elderly sister named Miss Groves, a British missionary who had been working in China for many years. She had a ministry with a certain gift for preaching the gospel. Regardless of how busy she was or what the weather was like, every day except the Lord's Day, after tea time at 3:00 P.M. she would bring a bundle of tracts and stand on the street. At that time she was about seventy years old. Eventually people testified that they were helped to know the Lord through her ministry. She did this in a weighty way, because she was a person with a burden.

In those years many Western missionaries went to China, especially young women in their twenties and early thirties. Whenever a group of new missionaries came to China, most of them would stay in Shanghai as their first station. This elderly sister would always invite the young female missionaries to her home, not to a big feast but for afternoon tea. On one occasion, almost all the young women had skirts above the knee. After serving tea, she sat down with them, and while sitting she kept adjusting her skirt over her legs, although her skirt was already long. After she did this two or three times, all the young women did the same thing. After that invitation to afternoon tea, all those young missionaries changed the style of their skirts. That was a real ministry to them.

This sister labored in the Lord and for the Lord for the long run. She did not dream that the Lord would give her power from on high; she simply labored in a normal way. If anyone visited her, they could sense the presence of the Lord, because she was a person who always labored. This was truly something for the Lord, and we heard many testimonies from those young missionaries, especially from the young women, as to how much help they received from her laboring in a normal way. In addition, many persons could say that they were saved through her labor. We need to be balanced, and we need to labor for the Lord over the long run.

CHAPTER FIVE

TEN WAYS TO PREACH THE GOSPEL

Scripture Reading: Hag. 1:7-9

In this chapter we shall continue to speak about having an outreach and reaching unbelievers.

THE PURPOSE OF GOSPEL PREACHING BEING TO BRING MATERIALS FOR THE BUILDING OF GOD'S HOUSE

Haggai 1:7 through 9 says, "Thus says Jehovah of hosts, Consider your ways. Go up to the mountain and bring wood and build the house, and I will take pleasure in it and will be glorified, says Jehovah. You looked for much, and yet it amounted to little; and when you brought it home, I blew on it. Why? declares Jehovah of hosts. Because of My house that lies waste while you each run to your own house." In Christianity there is much teaching to push people to do gospel work. However, the purpose of this gospel work is only to win souls. If we come back to the picture in Haggai, we will see that God's intention to bring in people is not merely on the negative side, to save their fallen soul from hell. Rather, it is something positive. God's intention is to bring more materials for the building of His house. We need God's salvation not only because we are fallen but because God has an eternal purpose to accomplish, and for this purpose there is the need for many persons as material. Therefore, we need to bring more people to the Lord as the materials.

The type of the temple is a clear picture of the building of the church. In the Old Testament time the people of Israel were charged to go to the mountain to bring material for the building of God's house. This type signifies that we must go out to reach unbelievers for the building of the house of God. If we have this understanding, aim, and burden in reaching people, our results will be one hundred percent different. We are not going out only to bring souls to be saved; we are going out to bring people as the dear, precious materials for the building of God's temple.

OUR NEED TO BE BALANCED IN LIFE AND NUMBERS

The brothers and sisters who have been raised up by the Lord in these days to take the way of His recovery must realize that we must always increase in two ways. We must increase in the measure of life, and we must also increase in the number of persons. This is to increase both in quality and quantity. To be increased in the growth and measure of life is to be increased in quality. However, quality always comes out of quantity. If we do not have the quantity, how can we have the quality? We need the quantity, the increase of numbers.

It is easy for Christians to be unbalanced and go to an extreme. We need to learn to be balanced in several directions. We need to grow in life, but we also must increase in number. Life always must grow in all the churches day by day, and our numbers also always must increase. Otherwise, we are unbalanced; we are a "cake not turned" (Hosea 7:8).

CHECKING OURSELVES BY THE INCREASE IN NUMBERS

It may be that in a local church the increase comes mainly from brothers and sisters who immigrate from the Far East. These believers are like children born in someone else's home; they are the "adopted children" of that local church. This means that as regards the increase, that church still has a failure.

It is not sufficient to bring only one person to the Lord every two years. Two years is too long; consider how many days and hours are in two years. This means that if we start with fifty persons, in two years we will have only one hundred, and in four years we will have two hundred. This may sound good, but it is not completely good. In Taiwan in 1949 we had close to a thirtyfold increase in only one year. We started with thirty to fifty people, and by the end of the year we had over one thousand.

If we cannot bring one person to the Lord in two years, there is little practical purpose to being on earth. On the earth, even in one large city, there are millions of people. In such an ocean of faces, why can we not bring one person to the Lord? We have very much neglected our duty. It is not right or fair to be on the earth for two years and not bring one person to the Lord. Sometimes, though, we are even worse than this; we may not have brought one person to the Lord in four years. I am concerned about this situation. Let us not criticize others; let us criticize ourselves.

The best way to check whether a commercial business is right or wrong is to look at its accounting. We should not care for the general manager's or director's report; we should check the accounting books. What is its balance, profit, loss, and liabilities, and what kind of turnover has it had in the past ten years? We should look at the statistics and worksheets. In the same way, we should not say that our meetings are wonderful and everything is wonderful. If everything is wonderful for a whole year, yet there is no increase, there must be something wrong. We need to check ourselves.

BEING BALANCED IN FIVE MATTERS

According to our training and experience in the church life, we have learned that we must stress the balance of five things: life, truth, service, gospel preaching, and going out for the gospel. The matter of life is very basic; we need life to grow. Then as regards the truth, we must be trained to know the word of the Scriptures in a proper, living way. The service is the Body life and includes the meetings and every kind of function and ministry in the church. Then we must also have gospel preaching. In addition to this, we need to go out for the gospel, not as apostles but simply as disciples. In Acts the first way for the spread of the gospel was not the way of apostles going out. It was the way of the disciples being scattered (Acts 8:1). The disciples were scattered by the persecution in Jerusalem, and wherever they went, they brought the gospel. That was the spreading of the gospel and the expanding of the kingdom of God. In order to go on with the Lord in the way of His recovery, we need to be balanced by stressing all the above matters.

HAVING BOTH
THE FISHING AND MENDING MINISTRIES

As we saw in a previous chapter, after the Lord was anointed to minister, he called two pairs of disciples, representing two kinds of ministries (Matt. 4:18-22). When the first pair was called, they were fishing by casting a net, and when the second pair was called, they were mending their nets. The fishing ministry is to bring people in, and the mending ministry is to keep them from falling out. The fishing ministry is to open the front door, while the mending ministry is to close the back door, to keep people in to be built up. Through Peter, who had the fishing ministry, the doors of the kingdom were opened (16:19). The keys of the kingdom were given to him, and he used them to bring people in. Today in the church there must be many Peters with the fishing ministry. Wherever they go, the door will be open, and they will bring people in.

Then after Peter brings people in, John follows with the mending ministry. People should only come in; they should not go out. They come in the front door and should not go out the back door. The back door has to be mended closed in order to keep people in until they are built up. Eventually the New Jerusalem comes out of the mending ministry. The one who wrote about the New Jerusalem was not Peter but John, who had the mending ministry. The fishing ministry is for the start, while the mending ministry is for the accomplishment. In the church we need these two ministries. Moreover, with these two ministries there is the possibility for the building, so between the fishing and the mending ministries there is the building ministry of Paul.

We must have the outreach. We must bring unbelievers to the Lord, spread the word of the gospel, and expand the kingdom of God. I would encourage you, even burden you, to take care of these matters. Otherwise, we are not balanced; we are wrong.

HAVING THE RIGHT WAY TO CATCH PEOPLE

After we are burdened, we will want to know the way to reach people, to "catch the fish." To do anything, we need certain ways. When a general leads an army to take a city, for example, he may take several ways. Depending on the situation, he may come from different directions. Moreover, one city should be taken in the morning, while another city should be taken at night; and one should be taken from the north, but another should be taken from the south. In the same way, to bring a person to the Lord we must have wisdom to know the proper time and the proper way. Here we can only give principles; you must practice them to learn the details.

The Way of Sin

According to our past experiences, there are at least ten ways to deal with a person for Christ. In order to catch people, we must realize what they are and where they are. The first way to catch people is with the matter of sin. This is not the only way, nor is it the best way, but it is one of the prevailing ways.

All people on the earth are sinful; they are sinners, and many are in a very bad situation of sin. However, it is not right to touch everyone by dealing with sin. It is only right if they are conscious that they are sinful and to some degree desire victory over and deliverance from their sin. If a person is like this, this is the best opportunity to use this way to catch him. We need to strike his conscience even the more. Such a one is already conscious that he is sinful, but we still need to make him more conscious of sin. This creates a hunger and thirst to be saved and a realization of how much he needs salvation and deliverance.

The most important thing for a salesman is to create a market. When there is a market, it is easy to sell, but if there is no market, no one will buy. We need to create the need within a sinner. For this purpose, we must know the best passages to use from the Scriptures. If we are familiar with the best passages, they will be ready and handy to us to deal with this kind of person.

There are two aspects of sin. One aspect is the nature of sin, and the other is the outward deeds of sin. We should be familiar with these two aspects and know how to deal with a person in both ways.

When we deal with a sinner, we should remember not to talk too much. Salesmen know the secret of making a deal and then not talking too much; if they talk too much, they will lose the deal. After making a deal, a salesman gets the buyer to sign and pay; for us this means that we ask the sinner to pray.

The Way of the Result of Sin

The second way to catch people is according to the result of sin. I would advise you not to use this way very much, but with some persons we must use this way. It always depends on what kind of person we are talking with. If a person is conscious of his sins and is more or less afraid of the result, we should take advantage of this. We may compare this to fighting a battle. We should not attack the stronghold; rather, we should find and attack the weak point. When we contact people, it is easy to find their weak point. If a person is afraid of death or has a consideration about the future, this is his weak point.

There are two kinds of suffering as the result of sin. One is the suffering in the present age, which we can illustrate to them. In the present age, one who sins in dancing, drinking, and gambling will suffer physically, financially, and in other ways. A gambler, for instance, will suffer in his health, have a loss in his business, and damage his family. In addition, one who drinks too much will shorten his life on the earth; he will die too quickly. The other kind of suffering as a result of sin is from the judgment and punishment after death, which we can show from the Scriptures. Again, we need to know the best verses of the Scriptures for this purpose.

The Way of the Vanity of Human Life

The third way to deal with people is according to the vanity of human life. This is almost the best way to contact people. Especially today people have the sense that human life is empty, nothing but a vanity of vanities. If we find that this is a person's weak point, we must take advantage and "attack." We need to point out that they sense the emptiness in human life because they do not have God and Christ. If they have Christ, they have God, and their life will be full and their sense of vanity will be swallowed up. However, they are short of Christ, so there is a gap in their life. The best verses to use for this purpose are from Ecclesiastes, which speaks of "vanity of vanities" (Eccl. 1:2).

The Way of God

The fourth way to catch people is according to God. Many people on the earth have a problem and question concerning God. They ask, "Is there a God? What have I to do with God?" When we talk with a person, we should sense whether he is one who has this sense about God, whether he fears God or desires to know God. For this, again we should know the best verses from the Bible.

The Way of the Love of God

The fifth way is according to the love of God. We should take this way with persons experiencing trouble, sickness, loss, and sufferings, persons who are disappointed, suppressed, and oppressed. We need to show such persons that God is love. This is one of the best ways. It is very easy to use this way to win people, but we must use it with the right people. We should not take this way with people who are rich and well off in many ways. It is when people are suffering that they need the love of God. Many times God prepares people's hearts by allowing them to suffer. When people suffer, it is easy for them to be won by the love of God.

The Way of Christ

The sixth way is the highest way, the way of Christ. However, this way is not easy to carry out. It is hard to preach the gospel with the subject of Christ. This is the highest standard for the gospel, but some people need this. The people of high class and standard, the highly cultured and educated people, have a certain philosophy of human life. If we talk with them about God or sin, they will not care. We should talk to them according to the Scriptures about Christ as the center of the universe, the central element of all things, the goal of God's plan, and the need of the human life. In this message we do not have the adequate time to speak about this subject in detail; we need an entire morning and evening for six months to study this matter.

We should not speak about sin, hell, or heaven to this kind of person. We can never convince such a person in this way. I have met some professors who told me in principle, "We are not so selfish. We do not care about hell. We want something high." I learned from them, and I changed my way. The subject of Christ is their weak point. We should simply speak about Christ as the goal, the aim, the standard, the center, the element, and all things. We should point out to them the highest standard and ultimate goal of life. Then we should give them the right passages of the Scriptures and the right illustrations. I have done this, and many people have been saved in this way. If we take this way, this kind of person will be won over.

The Way of the Redemption of Christ

The seventh way to catch people is according to the redemption of Christ. This is not the same as salvation; we must differentiate redemption from salvation. If we confuse these two, our preaching will not be prevailing. To confuse them is like selling one product but talking about another. We should concentrate on one matter. Redemption includes the cross of Christ, the blood of Christ, and the substitutionary death of Christ. In every place there are people who are conscious that they are sinful, and they are struggling and seeking a way to be saved. For people in this condition, we should preach in the way of redemption. We should lead them carefully and prove to them, even convince them, that nothing can save them but the redemption of Christ's cross through the shedding of His blood.

The Way of Life

The eighth way is the way of life. The way of Christ and the way of life are the two highest ways. It is very easy for Christians to preach the gospel in the way of sin and hell, but not many people are able to preach the gospel in the way of Christ or the way of life.

In the human community there are a number of thoughtful persons. Recently some brothers were invited to a sister's home for dinner. Her husband was a very thoughtful person. The brothers had a long talk with him concerning the Lord, but they were all defeated. He said that every man must do good, and he boasted much about his good deeds. I did not speak; rather, I watched and listened for his weak point. I did not argue with him about doing good. I simply told him, "It is wonderful to be such a person that does good," and then I pointed out to him that his life has a limitation. He can only do so much good; he cannot go further. His own life is a small tree that can bring forth only small fruit, so he needs a higher life. This point convinced him in the way of life.

The Way of Repentance by Faith

The ninth way is the way of repentance by faith. We must help people to repent to God and believe in the Lord Jesus. Many Christians do not have the assurance of salvation. We need to help them to know real repentance and exercise faith to take hold of the Word of God that they may have the assurance of salvation.

About forty years ago, almost no Christian in China had the assurance of salvation. The first battle that we fought in China was for this matter. Wherever we went, the first question we asked was, "Do you know that you have been saved?", and we always received a negative answer. Even the pastors would argue with us. At that time we were in our twenties. Some pastors said, "Young men, you are too proud. I have been a pastor for many years, but I don't know if I have been saved. This matter is in the Lord's hand. We must go on until one day we see Him. Let Him make the decision whether or not we are saved."

In 1933 I was invited to preach the gospel at a Presbyterian hospital near Shanghai. As I spoke about the assurance of salvation, I had to fight the battle because the pastor who sat in the rear kept shaking his head to disagree with me. This was a real battle in the early years in China, but after about ten years of fighting, the Christians there began to realize that once we believe in Christ according to the Word of God, we have the assurance of salvation. We still need this kind of preaching today.

The Way of Salvation

The tenth way to catch people is by the way of salvation. This way is not easy to take. We should take this way mostly by giving people a testimony about how certain persons were saved. This will help them to come to their own salvation.

NEVER ARGUING WHEN WE SPEAK WITH PEOPLE

Here I have given ten ways in a good order to catch people, but now you must do the "homework" to develop them. Concerning the technique, the secret of contacting people is never to argue with them. Rather, we should go along with them. Some brothers like to argue. When one person said that he had done many good things to help others, a brother replied that whatever we do means nothing; it can never be acceptable to God. This is an aspect of the truth, but we should not talk to people in this way. To speak to people in this way causes them to be in their mind. The best way is to reply, "That is right; we have to do good for others, and I am happy to hear that you do good for others. However, how much can we do? We can do only so much because we are limited by our capacity and ability. Our life is below the standard." This will convince a person and open his eyes to see the higher life.

We should not argue with people even about God. If someone says there is no God, we may say, "Perhaps you are right. If there were no God, that would save us from a lot of trouble; then we could do whatever we like. But suppose there is a God. What shall you do?" The secret of going along with people in this way is a small matter, but it is very effective. Sometimes a big machine without a little screw does not work; when we add the little screw, it works again. If we do not argue with people but go along with them, they will be caught.

CARING FOR TWO OR THREE UNBELIEVERS
AND INVITING THEM TO OUR HOMES

We should consider all the people we know and choose two or three unbelievers to care for the year round. We should not take care of too many. The best way to do this is to open our homes and invite them in. This is especially true for students. If we live on or close to a campus and have a way to contact people, it is easy to bring them to the Lord by inviting them to our home. Again, we should not invite too many, perhaps only two or three or even just one. Then we will know the best way to contact them. If we care for a certain one in this way and invite him to our home, he will be saved in half a year. Learn to do this.

DISTRIBUTING TRACTS AND BOOKLETS

There is also the need, especially for the young brothers and sisters, to have the habit of distributing tracts. We may do this on the street corner, on the bus, or other places. We should always have a tract or booklet in our pocket, and whenever there is the opportunity, we can give one to someone. This is a great help to our gospel preaching. This will create the atmosphere for preaching. A church should prepare a number of good tracts and booklets with the address of the meeting place, printing them in the thousands, and the brothers and sisters should take some of them in their pocket and distribute them wherever they go. This will bring people in.

PREACHING THE GOSPEL AND
HAVING A MEETING FOR THE GOSPEL

A church should also have gospel preaching on the street or in the park, not every day but once every one or two weeks. We also need a gospel preaching meeting of the church.

GOING ON IN A BALANCED WAY

A gospel preaching meeting, however, is not the most important matter. If we are not balanced, a meeting for the gospel will not work. Instead, all the regular attendants of the church meetings should care year round, on the one hand, for two or three unbelievers, and on the other hand, for two or three younger, weaker believers. If we always have someone under our care in this way, we will see how much we will learn and how much growth in life we will have. This will help us and cause us to seek the Lord. It will enlarge our heart and capacity, not to care for our business, family, home, studies, or future, but to care for others. We will experience the Spirit of Christ, and we will have the attitude and heart of Christ.

Life, truth, service, gospel, and going out for the gospel always work together. We should not say that we are too shallow and young in life, so we should concentrate our attention only on life. If we do this, we will not have much growth in life for even three, four, or five years. But if we pay attention not only to life but also to truth, to the church meetings and service, and to the gospel, we will rapidly grow in life. In the spiritual life as in the physical life there is the need of different aspects. To be healthy in the physical life we need food, clothing, housing, and hygiene. We cannot take only one of these aspects. It is the same with the spiritual life. Life, truth, service, gospel preaching, and going out for the gospel are all basically necessary.

I have the assurance that the Lord is merciful to us. If in addition to this we are faithful to Him, in no more than three years some brothers and sisters will go out for the purpose of the gospel. Some may go to the east coast, Canada, Mexico, or South America, not as missionaries but simply as disciples going out for the gospel. For the Lord's recovery we need to go out.

We cannot stay here merely meeting and talking in a spiritual way. If we do, the first year we may have fifty meeting with us, the next year fifty-one, the third year forty-nine, and the fourth year forty-five. If we lift up our standard too high, people will not come in. There are certain groups that speak much about spirituality, but after a few years their numbers are reduced. Finally everyone leaves because they cannot meet the high standard. This is one hundred percent wrong because it is unbalanced. A proper table needs four legs to be stable, and we also need to be balanced.

We all have to go on by the grace of God in the growth of life. We must know Christ as our life, know how to exercise our spirit, and know how to fellowship with Christ and contact Him not only day by day but also hour by hour. We also need to learn the lessons of the cross. These are the matters of life, but these are not all. If we have only these matters, we cannot grow properly; rather, we will be unhealthy. We also need to read the Word to know the truth in a living way. However, this is still not all. We also need the service. We need to come to the meetings to exercise, minister, contribute, function, and do everything we can to partake of the service. This also is a balance. In addition, we always need gospel preaching to bring people to the Lord. We should go to the street, the park, the city square, the schools, the factories, and to our businesses to do something for gospel preaching, the more the better. Still this is not all. Even life, truth, service, and the gospel are not sufficient or adequate. We also have to go out for the gospel.

Not all of us will go out for the gospel. Some will go, but all will follow them with prayer and even with the material supply. Then the Lord's kingdom will be expanded. This is the right way, and this is proof that we mean business with the Lord and we are not merely talking in a good way. If we do this, whatever the Lord has shown us will constantly increase, spread, and expand, as it did in the book of Acts.

Many Christians, including us, are not adequately balanced. To some degree, we go to one extreme or the other. May the Lord be merciful to us. We should not go to any extreme. We need to be balanced in several directions—in life, truth, service, gospel preaching, and in going out for the gospel. Therefore the church should stress that all the regular attendants do something for gospel preaching to reach unbelievers and to bring people to the Lord.

To be faithful in this matter, we must offer much prayer to the Lord, and we must be dealt with by the Lord. We may need to pray, "Lord, I cannot bring this person to You. Why is this?" We may be wrong or short in certain matters, so we must be dealt with, made right, and learn the lessons. Then we will know many things, not in speech only but in practice. This is the proper way for us to be balanced. If we do this, the church will be very much benefited, and we will gain the advantage to grow in life.

CHAPTER SIX

FOUR PRACTICAL POINTS
ON REACHING UNBELIEVERS

I have the deep burden that if we mean business to practice the Body life, the church life, we need a balance of five matters: life, truth, gospel, service, and going out to other places for the gospel. In order to truly practice the church life, we need these things. The first four matters—life, truth, gospel, and service—are very basic. Eventually, though, we need even the last item. Some of us need to go out to other places, and the prayer and finances of those who remain must follow them. In other words, our person, our heart, our prayer, and our money have to go out to reach other lands, other fields, for the Lord's kingdom and His interests. Then we will have the proper church life.

PRAYING FOR UNBELIEVERS

In this chapter we shall speak something more vital and practical concerning how to reach unbelievers. There are four matters about which we should be very clear and which we must put into practice in order to reach the unbelievers in a fruitful way. The first matter is prayer. A person who is fruitful in reaching unbelievers must be a praying person, a person of prayer. In a general way, we may say that we already know this. However, to know this is one thing, while to practice it is another. Even if some do practice prayer, they may not have the best secret of the practice of prayer. When we have the burden and the heart to reach unbelievers to bring them to the Lord, we must first learn how to pray for them.

Praying to Be Burdened for People's Souls

We need to go to the Lord to ask Him to burden us with this matter. We should ask the Lord to give us the burden to reach unbelievers. I believe that in these last days we all have a heart to realize the Lord's recovery. If we do, we must pray definitely for others and especially for ourselves, saying, "Lord, burden me for people's souls." This is the most important thing for the Lord's interests in these days. The Lord's house "lies waste" (Hag. 1:9), so there is the need of the recovery of the building. We cannot merely sit and talk about the building. For a building, there is the need of materials (v. 8). With what shall we build? If today we have twenty persons, next year we have eighteen, and the third year we have fifteen, we will eventually disband. For the building we need materials. In a similar way, a family needs children, the more the better. Therefore, we all must pray that the Lord would burden us. Keep this matter in mind, and go to the Lord concerning this. We all must put this kind of prayer into practice, even this very day or tomorrow morning at the latest. We should pray, "Lord, burden me with the souls for whom You died on the cross and with whom You will build up Your Body." I believe that the Lord will honor this prayer.

We should forget about our weakness. I am afraid that some of us have been praying too much about our own weakness. We are too self-centered, saying, "Oh, I am weak. O Lord, I lose my temper." It is always "I." Forget about this poor "I" and consider the Lord's interests. Look at all the souls. In a major city there are millions of people. Whenever I fly over Los Angeles, I look down from the plane at the city, and I have a great burden for it. What a big city it is; it takes the airplane fifteen minutes to cross it! The metropolitan area around Los Angeles has millions of people. It is a big "ocean" full of different kinds of "fish." That we could not or would not catch some of them is a real shame. Day by day we meet many "fish." We must be burdened to catch some for the Lord. Therefore, we must pray that the Lord would burden us for people's souls.

Praying for Leading
concerning Two or Three Definite Persons

After we pray for the burden, we must immediately pray for guidance. This means that we should pray that the Lord will give us some definite persons, such as our classmates, roommates, neighbors, relatives, and friends. We should not pray for too many. Rather, we should pray to seek the Lord's guidance and that He would give us two or three persons to care for at the present time.

Praying Definitely for the Persons
for Whom the Lord Burdens Us

After we receive the guidance, we should pray for these persons. This is the principle of the New Testament. A person can never be saved without someone praying for him or her. If we trace the record of the New Testament, the history of the church, and the stories of many saints, we will find this principle. We must realize that we were saved because someone prayed for us. I know who prayed for me to be saved; I am very clear about this.

We must take this burden. Because this is the New Testament time, God will never do anything directly by Himself, although He is able to. He does everything related to gospel preaching through us by our cooperation. God could send an angel to prepare Cornelius, but He would not send an angel to preach the gospel to him and his family (Acts 10:1-7). The angel came to Cornelius, but he did not preach the gospel because that was not within his limit; it was not his obligation. This obligation belongs to saved humans. Therefore, the angel told Cornelius that he had to send for Peter, who would have the word of salvation. God could send the angel to tell people how to find an evangelist, but He would not send the angel to preach to them.

The two books written by Luke—his Gospel and the Acts—are books of the preaching of the gospel. However, these two books give us many illustrations of prayer. Of the four Gospels, Luke gives the most illustrations of how the Lord Himself always prayed. Acts also is a book of prayer.

Before the first preaching by the church on the day of Pentecost, the disciples prayed for ten days (1:14). Everything that happened after that related to preaching also needed to be started by prayer. The work of going out from Antioch was started by prayer (Acts 13:2). In Acts 10, the call to preach came to Peter while he was praying (vv. 9-17). Ananias, the small disciple who was sent to confirm Saul of Tarsus, received the vision of the Lord's sending in prayer (9:10-11). If we read the book of Acts, we can see that this book of preaching is a book of praying.

We all must pray definitely by name for the persons for whom the Lord burdens us. Learn to do this. When Brother Watchman Nee was a young man studying in the first two years of college, he would fast during the whole day of Saturday for his preaching the next day. Within those one or two years, close to two hundred students were brought to the Lord, almost entirely through him. This was a small college of no more than three hundred highly qualified students. After those years, almost the entire college was stirred up. If someone went to the campus and the halls, he would see the students doing almost nothing but reading the Bible and kneeling to pray. This was a real revival, which was due more than ninety-five percent to the young Brother Nee. Every week he purposely gave up breakfast, lunch, and dinner to shut himself in his room to pray and read, and on the next day, he would carry out the preaching of the gospel. All those who were brought to the Lord were truly converted and changed in life. In 1922 these persons had gospel preaching campaigns. It was not in a so-called church building but on the street or in the court of a home. They had no seats; they would tell people that whoever came to listen to the gospel had to bring their own seat. This revival was due to the prayer of Brother Nee.

Try to have this kind of prayer. I have the full assurance that the easiest prayer for the Lord to answer is the prayer for sinners. I will not give any regulations, but I would suggest that we as Christians, especially the young brothers, should have one or two days a week separated for the purpose of being with the Lord to pray for sinners and for the gospel. On those days we should keep all our prayers on this one matter, to pray definitely for the gospel preaching and for the certain persons for whom the Lord has burdened us. Without this, our outreach will not be prevailing. We have to touch the throne. Do not think that gospel preaching is an easy matter. It is a real battle. The Lord Jesus told us clearly that we have to bind the strong man, who is the enemy Satan, in order to release the wealth usurped by his hand (Matt. 12:29). To release the precious souls from the usurping hand of Satan, we need to pray and touch the throne. To save a person from hell and the fallen situation is not a small thing. Therefore, we must pray.

DEALING WITH THE LORD, CONSECRATING OURSELVES, AND CLAIMING THE POWER FROM ON HIGH

Before we go out to reach unbelievers, to invite them to our homes, to contact them with the purpose of bringing them to the Lord, we must have a definite dealing with the Lord. This dealing is of two aspects. First, we must deal with our sins and worldliness and consecrate ourselves to the Lord again for the purpose of gospel preaching. If we sincerely mean our consecration, the Lord will point out our sins and worldliness. Then we will need to deal with these things and make a thorough confession. We will tell the Lord that we give up all the things that He condemns. To deal with the sins and worldliness that the Lord points out to us is the real consecration.

Second, this kind of consecration is for power. After we consecrate in this way and gladly deal with all our sins and worldliness, we must claim the power from on high. We should not pay much attention to our experience, feelings, or the so-called manifestations of power. We should leave experience, feelings, and manifestation in the hands of the Lord and simply claim the power from on high by faith. We must not care whether or not we have tongues of fire upon us or other phenomena. Rather, we must simply consecrate ourselves to the Lord, be willing to deal with all the things He condemns, and claim His power by faith. Otherwise, we will not be prevailing.

When we claim the power from on high by faith, we will have authority. Many times I have asked people who claim to have the Pentecostal experience where their power is. They may say that their speaking in tongues is genuine, but where is the power? We must have the power. If we do not have power, we need to doubt our experience. I have seen and experienced to some extent that the only prevailing way to exercise the power from on high is to consecrate ourselves and claim the power. Then we may not have one bit of manifestation, but we will have the power, even if we cannot sense it. This power can be realized only by our consecration, our willingness to deal with whatever the Lord condemns, and our claiming of the power by faith.

We cannot have this kind of dealing once for all. Whenever we go to contact people, even twice a day, morning and evening, we must consecrate ourselves and claim the power from on high. Before 1949 I did much work of preaching. In north China at every New Year, we had a four-day gospel campaign. About a hundred people were brought in through those four days. The preaching of the church was truly prevailing and powerful. I would always give the message, and the church would care for the other matters. The whole church shared the burden. In those days I did nothing but pray, "Lord, here I am. Empower me. Whatever You condemn, I condemn too." Then I claimed the power by faith. I cannot tell you what kind of power we had! That preaching was truly powerful. If you had been there, you would have seen the power. The meetings were prevailing. Even the unbelievers in the market and on the street would say that no one could come into our building without being struck down, not physically but by the spiritual power. One could sense the power there. By this experience, I learned that whenever we go to contact people, we have to pray. In those years we did much work of visitation for those unbelievers who came to attend the gospel meeting. Whenever we did this kind of work, we needed to pray definitely, consecrate ourselves to the Lord, deal with the things which the Lord condemned, and then claim the power from on high. What I am speaking is a training, not merely a message. If we do not take these things and put them into practice, we will get nothing.

SPEAKING LIVING WORDS WITH THE LORD'S GUIDANCE

The third practical point for reaching unbelievers is that when we go to contact people, we should speak things not merely according to our memory but by contacting the Lord. In our gospel preaching we must learn to speak not by what we know or by what we decide to say. Rather, we should keep ourselves open, and while we are speaking, we should fellowship with the Lord to speak living words according to the inner guidance. We also do not need to keep a good order when we speak. We can never help people to be saved merely by keeping an orderly speaking. This is the way of the lecturer, professor, or teacher in a classroom.

When we contact people to preach the gospel, our speaking may jump around. Once when I was preaching from the platform, I suddenly pointed to a young student and said, "You stole chalk from the school." That had nothing to do with my message. However, the boy later testified that he had actually done such a thing. When I spoke in this way, he was surprised and told himself that it did not mean anything. Then I said, "You are saying that this does not mean anything." I continued, "You brought the chalk home and drew circles on the floor." This was exactly what he had done. That young boy was trembling, and he was saved. His mother was one of the deaconesses in the church. The next morning when I went into the deacon's office, she was there. She was very glad, saying, "Brother Lee, that was a real miracle. How did you know he stole chalk from the school? How did you know that he said to himself that it meant nothing, and how did you know that he brought the chalk home and drew circles on the floor?" I do not know how I knew. That was simply my preaching. This illustrates that when we go to preach the gospel to people, we should forget about mere doctrine and a good order in our speaking.

Learn to do this. It is not an easy matter. Watchman Nee said, "We always like to keep our message and forget about souls. We must realize that we are sent by the Lord to save souls, not to save our message." This is one hundred percent right. However, many times in our preaching we save our message and keep it in a good sequence. Then people may say that our message is nice, but they will go to hell. It is not a matter of a nice message; it is a matter of the saving power.

In our speaking we need the living word. My older sister, who worked for the Lord, told me about Dr. John Sun. When he was preaching the gospel to a large congregation in the middle of China, the heartland, to a crowd of one thousand people, he suddenly pointed to a young lady in the crowd and said, "You are a concubine." That was the first time this young lady had come to hear Christian preaching. She was thoroughly offended, but in actuality she was a concubine. The Holy Spirit convicted and convinced her by that speaking, and she came to the Lord. I can give many stories like this to illustrate how we must learn to speak with people about the gospel in a living way, not according to mere knowledge and doctrine.

LEARNING TO USE THE SCRIPTURES
IN A VITAL, PRACTICAL, AND LIVING WAY

We must also learn to use the word of the Scriptures in a vital, practical, and living way. First we pray for people, claim the power from on high, and speak to them in a living way. In this way we come to the point at which we can bring them to be saved. At this point we must "close the deal," just as a salesman does. In gospel preaching the way to close the deal is to use the Word. In the past years I have noticed that many brothers and sisters speak with people in a good way about the gospel, but they are short of closing the deal by using the proper passage of the Word. This is very important. When we speak with people, we come to a certain point at which we should not talk any more; we should simply use the Word to close the deal. This is just like a salesman when he brings a person to the point of asking him to sign the contract.

Nearly everyone is familiar with John 3:16, but we may not know how to use it properly. We may talk with a person and bring him to the point where he realizes God's love and that he needs the Son of God. At this point, he may not be clear whether or not he is saved. Then we must use a passage like John 3:16. This verse is very familiar to us, yet we must use it in a living way to close the deal. We may compare this verse to a knife. A knife may be sharp, but we need the right technique to properly cut with it. This verse says, "For God so loved the world that He gave His only begotten Son, that every one who believes into Him would not perish, but would have eternal life." After reading this verse with someone, we may ask him what it says, and by repeating it to us he will be impressed. We may ask him, "Do you realize whose word this is?" This will help him to realize that this is the word of God. We can then illustrate that even we as gentlemen keep our word. To be sure, God will keep His word. Then we can point out item after item of the verse in a living way to impress him: God loved, He gave, we believe, we have, and we will not perish. We can ask him to change the pronoun in the verse and read it two or three times as, "For God so loved me that He gave me His only begotten Son, that if I believe into Him, I will not perish, but will have eternal life." Then we can ask, "Do you have eternal life? Will you perish?" Right away he may tremble and say, "Praise the Lord, I have the eternal life and I will not perish!"

The Word is living. To be sure, if we put the Word into people and help them to apprehend it in a living way, they will be saved by this word. The Holy Spirit who works within people will honor this, and we ourselves will honor the Word of God and make it real. Learn to use the Word in a living way.

A dear brother among us who was an eye specialist became one of the leading elders in the church in Shanghai and was imprisoned by the Communists until his death. As a young doctor in his hospital, he saw a patient, an elderly lady, and spoke with her about the gospel. He asked her if she was a believer, and she said that she was; she had come to know Jesus when she was a child. The doctor asked her, "Do you know that you have been saved?" She replied, "How can I know this? I simply believe in Jesus, and whether or not I shall be saved is in His hands. After I die, I will go to Him. If

He says I am saved, I will be saved, but if He says I am not, I will perish." The young doctor opened John 3:16 to her and asked her if she knew it. She said that she was taught to recite it from her youth. He asked her to recite it and then told her that she had recited it wrongly; perhaps nine out of ten people recite verses wrongly. He told her that she was saying, "For God so loved the world that He gave His only begotten Son, that every one who believes into Him must wait for many years to see the Lord and be told by Him that he will not perish but have eternal life." She laughed at this, but he asked, "What does your John 3:16 say?" In this way that elderly woman was saved that night. She was very happy, saying, "Now I know that God loved, God gave, I believe and receive, I have eternal life, and I will not perish." We may give a hundred messages to help people in a general way, but to spend five minutes to give someone a passage of the Word in a living way helps them to be definitely saved. Learn to use the verses of the Scriptures in a living and practical way.

A co-worker named Brother Chang went to visit a person who was deathly ill. This person had a certain amount of Christian knowledge. The brother realized that this man was at the very point where he could be helped by a living word from a definite verse of the Scriptures; he was trained in this way and knew how to use the Word. The book of 1 John is not mainly for the gospel, but the brother realized that the ill man was very condemned in his conscience, so he used this book to preach the gospel. Brother Chang asked him if he would like to believe in the Lord, to which the man said yes. The brother closed the deal by asking him to pray, but the man did not know how to pray. He told him simply to say, "Lord, I am a sinner. You died on the cross for me, so I believe in You and receive You as my Savior." However, the man still said, "I am a sinful person. Throughout my whole life I have wronged persons too much, and now my conscience condemns me with all those things. I have prayed, but what about my sins?" Brother Chang read 1 John 1:7b and 9, which say, "The blood of Jesus His Son cleanses us from every sin....If we confess our sins, He is faithful and righteous to forgive us our sins and cleanse us from all unrighteousness." He said, "This is the word of God. God will never take back His word. He has to keep it." He asked the ill man to read the verses a few times and change the pronouns to *I* and *me:* "The blood of Jesus His Son cleanses me from every sin....If I confess my sins, He is faithful and righteous to forgive me my sins and cleanse me from all unrighteousness." The man said, "Thank God! He forgives me and has cleansed me." These verses were wrought into him, the Holy Spirit honored this word, and the man was saved.

We should not talk too much with people. If we talk with someone for half a day, we may not close the deal with him. Rather, we should speak in a very brief, practical, living, and real way. We all must learn to do this. We may also use 1 John 5:11, which says, "And this is the testimony, that God gave to us eternal life and this life is in His Son." We may tell people, "This is not a word in the air; it is a testimony. A testimony cannot be changed. The eternal life that God gives us is Christ." Then we can read verse 12, which says, "He who has the Son has the life; he who does not have the Son of God does not have the life," and we can ask, "Do you have life?" A person may reply, "I do not know," so we can ask, "This verse says that he who has the Son has the life. Do you have Christ the Son?" If the person is still not clear, we can ask him to receive the Lord by praying, and if he says he does not know how to pray in this way, we can tell him to say in a simple way, "Lord, I realize that I do not have eternal life. Eternal life is in You. Now I believe in You and receive You as my Savior." At this point if we ourselves pray for him, that indicates that we do not believe. There is no need for us to pray. We should simply believe what he prayed and ask him to read verse 12: "He who has the Son has the life." Then we can help him to realize that since he has prayed to receive the Lord, he now has the Son and therefore has the life. Verse 13 continues, "I have written these things to you that you may know that you have eternal life, to you who believe into the name of the Son of God." We can read this and ask, "Do you know that you have eternal life?", to which he should say, "Praise the Lord, I know by this word that I have eternal life!"

We can use many good verses to close the deal. We can use

Isaiah 53 to speak a hundred different messages in a practical, living way. Verse 6 says, "We all like sheep have gone astray; / Each of us has turned to his own way, / And Jehovah has caused the iniquity of us all / To fall on Him." We can read this to someone and explain, "To the Lord we are like sheep who have gone astray and turned to our own way. God has laid our iniquity on Him. Who is 'Him?' It is Christ the Savior. God has laid our sins on Him. What about you? Do you realize that you are like a sheep who has gone astray?" Again, we can ask him to read the verse and change the pronouns: "I like a sheep have gone astray; / I have turned to my own way, / And Jehovah has caused my iniquity / To fall on Him." In this way we can work this verse into the person, and he will be saved. Such a brief word is much better than a long message. We need to believe that the Word of God is powerful.

If we learn to use the verses of the Scriptures in a living way, we will know what verse is fit for certain persons. Acts 13:39 is a verse on justification. It says, "And from all the things from which you were not able to be justified by the law of Moses, in this One everyone who believes is justified." We can explain this verse briefly to someone by saying, "You cannot justify yourself by keeping the law, that is, by doing good. But if you believe in Jesus, you will be justified by Him from all things." We can read this verse, and then we should ask the other person to read it. Acts 10:43 is a verse about the forgiveness of sins: "To this One all the prophets testify that through His name everyone who believes into Him will receive forgiveness of sins." This illustrates how we should use different verses for different persons. We need to practice this and find the most prevailing verses.

Another verse is Romans 1:19, which says, "Because that which is known of God is manifest within them, for God manifested it to them." Sometimes people argue that it is hard to know God. We can read this verse to them and ask, "Don't you have a sense or feeling within you about God? If there is no God, why is there condemnation and fear within you when you are about to do something evil? God is manifesting something of Himself within you." In this way we can feed their conscience within them. We can continue with verse 20, which says, "For the invisible things of Him, both His eternal power and divine characteristics, have been clearly seen since the creation of the world, being perceived by the things made, so that they would be without excuse." Then we can add, "We can say, 'Excuse me,' to people, but we cannot excuse ourselves before God; we have no excuse." To use a living passage of the Scriptures in a practical way is better than giving a long message. However, this depends on our technique, and technique depends on practice. We need to practice.

When Watchman Nee was young, he had many experiences of gospel preaching. Once while he was still in school, five or six brothers tried to deal with one person. That person was not completely against the gospel. He had a certain intention to be saved, but all those brothers fought with him for hours without getting through. Eventually they came to Brother Nee, who was sick in bed, and told him the story. Brother Nee asked them to bring that person to him. When that person came to Brother Nee, he was saved right away. The five or six brothers worked for hours without getting through, but with Brother Nee he was saved immediately. This indicates the real need for practice.

The four foregoing main points are the main things that can help us to be very prevailing in the outreach to unbelievers in gospel preaching. We need to pray, claim the power, learn to speak with people not according to our mere knowledge, and eventually close the deal by using the proper verse in a proper way. There is almost no exception to this way. We must learn to do this.

BEARING FRUIT IN A DETAILED WAY

As we saw in the previous message, there are at least ten ways to speak to people about the gospel. These are the ways of:

1) sin,
2) the result of sin,
3) the vanity of human life,
4) God,
5) the love of God,
6) Christ,

7) the redemption of Christ,
8) life,
9) repentance by faith, and
10) salvation.

These points are easy if we consider their order. We are sinful, and with sin there is an issue, a consequence, a result. Human life is vain and empty, but we have God, His love, and His Christ. Because of the redemption of Christ through the cross, we have life, which we receive through repentance by faith. The result of repentance by faith is salvation. We need to use these ten points to "attack" people with the gospel; we must be an army to defeat Satan by hitting people's weak point.

We need to learn these things. It is not too hard; rather, it is easy if we practice. I beg you to practice this. Otherwise, it will be difficult to have the real increase. The gospel must be preached in this way by the living members of the Body. We should not depend much on the so-called great evangelists. We must depend on the members of the Body.

The fruit spoken of by the Lord in John 15, that is brought forth by the branches of the vine, are the souls saved through us. As the branches of the vine, we must bear fruit; that is, we must produce new believers. In a general way we need to abide in Christ to bear fruit. But in a detailed way we need to pray, claim the power from on high, learn to speak to people in a living way, not merely according to our memory, and learn to use the Lord's word in a living, practical way. Then it will be very easy to bear fruit. We will be the branches bearing fruit all the time. I expect that in one year we will see the number among us increase. Otherwise, there must be something wrong. To be sure, this will mean that we are wrong in certain aspects. To not be fruitful means that we are wrong. May the Lord be merciful to us.

OUR NEED FOR TRAINING

If we take this word merely as a message, it will not and cannot help us much. This is a training to instruct us how to practice. If we do not practice, this word will mean nothing. However, if we do practice it, we will appreciate this training more and more. When many saints in the Far East first came to be trained, they asked me not to be very strict with them, but after ten years they said that I had not been strict enough. I have learned these matters, and in this way I have come to know that we need training. Paul told Timothy, "For bodily exercise is profitable for a little, but godliness is profitable for all things, having promise of the present life and of that which is to come" (1 Tim. 4:8). We have to exercise in the spiritual things and learn to practice.

THE NEED FOR HUMAN COOPERATION

Many Christians today are superstitious, saying, "Everything is all right. The Lord will do it all." Everything is not all right. We have our part and must take care of our obligation. We need to cooperate with the Lord. The principle of the New Testament is that the Lord never does things by Himself; rather, He always does things with us. He needs the human cooperation. If we do not cooperate, He cannot do what He wants. He said the gospel would be preached to the uttermost part of the earth, but almost two thousand years have passed, and this word is still not fulfilled. Is He not able? He is more than able, but He has delayed for this long because the New Testament principle is that He needs human cooperation. By Himself in His old creation He said, "Let there be light," and there was light, but in His new creation He needs human cooperation. He Himself needed to be incarnated, to put on the human nature. Whatever Christ did, He did it in the principle of incarnation.

The reason the Lord has delayed so long is that it is very hard for Him to have the human cooperation. How much He will do and can do depends on how much cooperation we render to Him. To be sure, if we render Him more and more cooperation, He will do more. Today the secret is not with the Lord; it is with us. We need to bear our responsibility. With Him there is no problem, but we may not be ready. Therefore, we have to practice and give Him the adequate human cooperation. Then He will work.

CHAPTER SEVEN

THE CENTRAL PURPOSE OF THE GOSPEL

Scripture Reading: John 3:3, 5-6, 16, 36; Acts 11:18; 13:46, 48;
Rom. 5:10, 17-18; 6:4; 1 Cor. 4:15; Eph. 2:5; Titus 3:5; James
1:18; 1 Pet. 1:3, 23; 2:2; 1 John 1:1-3; 5:11-13

When we contact unbelievers to bring them to Christ and
help them to be saved, we must be very clear about the central
point of the gospel, God's main purpose in saving people and
bringing them to Himself in Christ. We have pointed out ten
ways to contact people for the gospel, but regardless of which
way we take, we must keep the goal in mind. The way is for
the goal. The ten ways are not the goal; there is only one
goal. The goal of the gospel is life. We need to bring people to
Christ because people need to have the life of Christ.

THE CENTRAL POINT
OF GOD'S SALVATION BEING LIFE

In the entire Scriptures God's intention is to give Himself
to people as life. What we humans need is the life of God, that
is, God Himself as our life. We have to stress this very much,
because in today's Christianity life is mostly neglected.
Rather, the gospel in Christianity is mostly along the line of
peace, happiness, eternal blessings, justification, and salvation. It is hard to hear a message of the gospel on the central
point of God's economy, which is life. We believe that the Lord
will recover this matter today.

Whenever we bring someone to the Lord, we should help
him or her to realize that the central point of God's salvation
is life. Why does a person need to be justified? It is because
justification is for life; without justification we cannot receive
life. Why should a person be cleansed? It is because cleansing

is for life; without cleansing, the divine life cannot be imparted into a person. Why do we need God's redemption? It is because we need life, and it is through redemption that we receive life from God. Neither justification, redemption, cleansing, holiness, nor sanctification is the goal; they are the process for the goal, which is life.

Life is eternal. It is not something merely in time. It is of eternity because from eternity and for eternity God's intention is to impart Himself as life into man. After God's creation of man, God put man in front of the tree of life with the intention that man would receive Him as life. We need to receive food day by day, whether or not we have been dirty. Even if we never become dirty, we still have to receive food. In the same way, even if man had never fallen, he was still made as a vessel to receive God as life. This is the central intention of God. Christianity today, however, neglects the central aim and intention of God and pays its full attention to the mending aspect. Justification and redemption are the mending aspect; they are not the original intention of God. I am stressing this because from now on the gospel preaching of the church must be in a way that is different from the way of today's Christianity. The way of our preaching must be the recovery of the ancient way.

God created man with the intention to put Himself into man as life. Then man became fallen, and God came in to bring him back. In this bringing back, God did something to cleanse, redeem, and justify man. He even separated man because man had fallen into the world of Satan, into the devil's system. This separation is sanctification. However, cleansing, redemption, justification, and sanctification are not the goal. The goal is life. Cleansing, redemption, justification, and sanctification are all for life. If man had never fallen, there would have been no need for cleansing, redemption, justification, and sanctification, but there would still have been the need for life.

We may illustrate God's intention with a soft drink bottle. The purpose of a soft drink bottle is to receive the soft drink and be filled with it. Before the bottle is filled, however, a naughty boy may dirty and damage the bottle. Now the owner has to recover it, clean it, and separate it from the trash.

However, the recovering, cleaning, and separating are not the aim; they are merely the process. After the bottle is recovered, there is still the need to fill it with the soft drink. The aim and goal are to fill the bottle.

In the gospel of God, the central matter is that man has to receive Christ as life. Man needs to have life through Christ, in Christ, and by Christ. However, we may have been impressed, even indoctrinated, by our background of Christianity. Because of this, whenever we speak about the gospel, we forget about life and pay too much attention to justification, redemption, and sanctification. Even worse, we may pay our attention to bringing people to go to heaven. Going to heaven is the worst concept. I cannot find a verse in the New Testament that tells us that the gospel is for people to go to heaven. I challenge you to tell me which of the twenty-seven books of the New Testament, and which chapter and verse, tell us that the gospel is for bringing people to heaven. Let us forget about this background and come back to the New Testament to see the central point of the gospel.

THE CENTRAL POINT OF THE FOUR GOSPELS

In the New Testament we first have the four Gospels. Matthew deals with the kingdom of the heavens, showing that the fallen human race is rebellious to the heavenly rule. How can man, having a rebellious life and nature, be subject to the heavenly rule and reign of the kingdom? It is not possible for us to experience Matthew 5 through 7. We cannot truly love our enemies because we do not have such a life (5:44). Our life is a hating life, not a loving life. It is a rebellious life, not a subjecting life.

It is not easy to say what the Gospel of Mark deals with, but if we carefully and thoroughly read this short book of sixteen chapters, we will see the example of a man on the earth who always forgets about Himself and His needs to always take care of God's interests. He is concerned for God's interests and lives for God's interests, not for His own things. For the sake of God's interests He even gave up His own eating (3:20).

According to the order of the books of the New Testament, Matthew comes first and Mark follows. In Matthew there is the subjection needed for the kingdom of the heavens, and in Mark there is the absolute obedience. Obedience is more than subjection. Someone may be subject to a certain person, yet he may not be willing to be obedient to him. Many children, for example, are forced to subject themselves to their parents, but they are not very willing to be obedient. Daniel's three friends were subject to the government of Nebuchadnezzar, but they were not obedient to his decree (Dan. 3:12). The brothers in a brothers' house may also be subject without being obedient. To God, therefore, subjection is one thing, while obedience is another. How can we humans be obedient? Again it is impossible because we do not have such a life. Our life and nature are completely disobedient.

It is also hard to know the subject of Luke unless we touch the spirit of this book. Some may check with expository books and say that Luke tells us that the Lord Jesus is a perfect and complete man, but this may be a mere doctrine. The real matter dealt with in the Gospel of Luke is man's harmony with God. In each of the twenty-four chapters of this book there is a man who is one hundred percent in harmony with God. This harmony is more than perfection and completeness. We may have subjection and even obedience to God, but it is possible that we do not have harmony with God. Harmony with God is deeper and finer. A person cannot be fully subject and obedient until he is harmonious with God. Harmony comes from full obedience, and full obedience comes from full subjection. In the book of Luke, the man by the name of Jesus was harmonious with God in everything. There was not one thing with Him that was contradictory to God. Because He was so harmonious with God, He was a perfect and complete man.

To be a person with such subjection, obedience, and harmony with God is possible only when we come to the fourth Gospel, the Gospel of John, which deals with life. Now we have subjection, obedience, harmony, and life. Until life is ministered to us by the Gospel of John, we can never be subject to the heavenly rule, obedient to God, and in harmony with God. All these items require life. To be subject, obedient, and harmonious requires us to receive Jesus Christ as our life. This life is the subjecting life, the obedient life, and the life in harmony with God. This shows us that life is the central item of the gospel.

THE PREACHING OF LIFE IN THE ACTS

Following the four Gospels, from the Acts to the end of the New Testament, there is the preaching of life, the teaching of life, and the ministering of life. It is all a matter of life. Since the Gospel of John is a Gospel of life, it is easy to find verses there that speak of life, such as verses 16 and 36 of chapter three. However, the Acts also shows us that the preaching in the early days of the apostles was a preaching of and for life. Acts 13:46 and 48 say, "And Paul and Barnabas spoke boldly and said, It was necessary for the word of God to be spoken to you first. Since you thrust it away and do not judge yourselves worthy of eternal life, behold, we turn to the Gentiles....And the Gentiles, hearing this, rejoiced and glorified the word of the Lord; and as many as were appointed to eternal life believed." By this we can see that the apostles preached the eternal life to people. Acts 11:18 is even clearer. After Peter related his account of the house of Cornelius, the disciples "became silent and glorified God, saying, Then to the Gentiles also God has given repentance unto life."

LIFE BEING THE CENTRAL POINT OF THE GOSPEL IN ROMANS THROUGH REVELATION

After the Acts, there are four main ministers in the New Testament: Paul, James, Peter, and John. The books from Romans to Revelation were written by these four plus Jude. In the ministry of Paul, James, Peter, and John life is the central point of the gospel.

The Generating Life in the Writings of Paul

In Paul's writings there are many verses that speak of the generating life. Ephesians 2:5 says, "Even when we were dead in offenses, made us alive together with Christ." This refers to our regeneration by Christ's resurrection. Similarly, Titus 3:5 says, "Not out of works in righteousness which we did but according to His mercy He saved us, through the washing of regeneration and the renewing of the Holy Spirit." Romans 5:10 says, "For if we, being enemies, were reconciled to God through the death of His Son, much more we will be saved in His life, having been reconciled." In addition, 1 Corinthians 4:15 says, "For though you have ten thousand guides in Christ, yet you do not have many fathers; for in Christ Jesus I have begotten you through the gospel." This shows us that when a person truly preaches the gospel to others, he is begetting them. I am stressing these matters because I would like to make it clear that in the early days, when the apostles went out to preach the gospel, their thought and intention was to beget people, that is, to impart life to them that they could be regenerated.

Romans 5:17 and 18 say, "For if by the offense of the one death reigned through the one, much more those who receive the abundance of grace and of the gift of righteousness will reign in life through the One, Jesus Christ. So then as it was through one offense unto condemnation to all men, so also it was through one righteous act unto justification of life to all men." Justification is not for itself; it is for life to be given to us, and through righteousness by justification we can reign in life. Romans 6:4 says, "We have been buried therefore with Him through baptism into His death, in order that just as Christ was raised from the dead through the glory of the Father, so also we might walk in newness of life." To walk in newness of life means that we have received life.

Being Brought Forth by the Word of Truth in James

The writings of James comprise only one book. James 1:18 speaks of regeneration, saying, "He brought us forth by the word of truth, purposing that we might be a kind of firstfruits of His creatures." Expositors speak much about this book, but they mostly neglect this verse that tells us that God begot us, regenerated us, by the word of truth.

Regeneration as the New Birth in the Writings of Peter

First Peter 1:3 says, "Blessed be the God and Father of our Lord Jesus Christ, who according to His great mercy has regenerated us unto a living hope through the resurrection of Jesus Christ from the dead." Verse 23 continues, "Having been regenerated not of corruptible seed but of incorruptible, through the living and abiding word of God." Similarly, 2:2 says, "As newborn babes, long for the guileless milk of the word in order that by it you may grow unto salvation." *Newborn babes* implies regeneration as the new birth, which Peter stresses.

The Preaching of the Eternal Life in the Writings of John

As we know, John 3:3, 5, and 6 speak of being born again. In addition, 1 John 1:1 through 3 says, "That which was from the beginning, which we have heard, which we have seen with our eyes, which we beheld and our hands handled, concerning the Word of life (and the life was manifested, and we have seen and testify and report to you the eternal life, which was with the Father and was manifested to us); that which we have seen and heard we report also to you that you also may have fellowship with us, and indeed our fellowship is with the Father and with His Son Jesus Christ." The apostles preached the eternal life which they had heard, seen, and handled. Verses 11 through 13 of chapter five say, "And this is the testimony, that God gave to us eternal life and this life is in His Son. He who has the Son has the life; he who does not have the Son of God does not have the life. I have written these things to you that you may know that you have eternal life, to you who believe into the name of the Son of God." This also shows us that the ministry in the early days was a ministry of life. The preaching, teaching, and ministry of the apostles was to preach life, teach life, and minister life.

HELPING PEOPLE TO REALIZE THAT THEY HAVE RECEIVED CHRIST AS LIFE

When we bring a person to the Lord, for the most part we

should not start with the matter of life. We need to start from something else, such as sin, the vanity of human life, or another item. However, we must keep in mind the goal of life. We have to bring people to life and help them to realize that to believe in the Lord Jesus as our Savior is to receive Him as our life. Unless we help people to realize that they have received Christ as their life, our work with them is not yet completed. Therefore, after we bring people to the Lord, we need to continue to spend time to help them to realize how the Lord Himself is life to us. Here we must explain to them that the Lord is the Spirit (2 Cor. 3:17; 1 Cor. 15:45b). Today it is easy to use electricity or atomic power to illustrate what the life within is. We should explain that God is Spirit, Christ is the Spirit, and God and Christ are in the Spirit waiting for us to receive Him and contact Him as life. We should also help them to realize that we are vessels made by God with a spirit within to receive God.

We must learn to do this. I am afraid that we may bring people to the Lord, but they may be saved without realizing that they have received Christ as life, that they have been born again, and that they have One living within them. This requires more work after we bring them to the Lord. Of course, this also requires our own experience. We must experience Christ as life to us, and then we will know how to help people to realize the same thing. The proper burden is not only to bring people to the Lord to be saved, but to bring them to the Lord that they may realize that today Christ is life to them, that they have a spirit within them, and that when they repent and believe in the Lord Jesus, the Holy Spirit works in their spirit to regenerate them and to bring Christ as the life-giving Spirit into their spirit.

To help people realize Christ as their life requires not merely that we give them doctrine but that we have a certain amount of experience. Second, it requires that we have the adequate verses from the Scriptures, such as those we have pointed out. We need to spend time on these verses to read, re-read, meditate, and pray about them until they become living to us. Then, when we contact people and help them to realize that Christ is their life, we will be able to use all those verses in a living way.

HELPING THE NEW BELIEVERS
TO EXERCISE THEIR SPIRIT

As we have pointed out, to help people to realize Christ as life should not be the beginning of our gospel preaching. Rather, it is the end, the conclusion. With many people we should not start with life; we should start in some other way. However, whatever way we take, we need to remember that we must bring people to the goal of life. Unless we help people to realize that they have Christ within as their life, and unless they know how to exercise their spirit to contact Christ as their life, our preaching of the gospel is not complete.

Some may say that to help new believers to know how to exercise their spirit is too much. We have been helped to know this for a long time, but many of us are still not clear how to exercise our spirit. However, although it may not be easy for us, it is easy for new believers. Some new believers will go on very quickly, more quickly than we have. We may illustrate this with learning English. When many old Chinese come to America, they are slow in learning the language, but their children learn quickly. The grandchildren speak English in a marvelous way, but the old grandfathers still cannot speak well because they have been spoiled by their old way of speaking. Similarly, many of us have been spoiled by our old way. I hope this word does not disappoint you, but many have been spoiled by being taught too much. It would have been better if they had never been taught so much. However, it is precious that many of us still have a right heart. If someone does not have a right heart, we cannot do anything with him. Many of us do have a right heart, but we also have oldness. We need the newness.

When we go out to preach the gospel in this new way, we will see some newborn babes who will go on in a fast way. We must not pass on the old way to them. If we pass on the old way, we pass on oldness. Therefore, regardless of which way we contact them to bring them to the Lord, we must right away help them to realize life. Do not think, "To exercise the spirit is too deep. How can they know this?" In actuality, they will understand it better than we do. Perhaps they will exercise more than we do, and after two months they will come back to teach us something. This is like the Chinese grandchildren who come back to teach the grandfather.

We should not set up ourselves as the examples, because we may not be good examples. We should set up the example from the Scriptures, telling them that on the very day or night they repented and believed in the Lord Jesus they already exercised their spirit to receive Him. Now the Lord is living, available, and real to them, for He is in them, that is, in their spirit. Romans 10:6 through 9 says, "But the righteousness which is out of faith speaks in this way, 'Do not say in your heart, Who will ascend into heaven?' that is, to bring Christ down; or, 'Who will descend into the abyss?' that is, to bring Christ up from the dead. But what does it say? 'The word is near you, in your mouth and in your heart,' that is, the word of the faith which we proclaim, that if you confess with your mouth Jesus as Lord and believe in your heart that God has raised Him from the dead, you will be saved." The reality of these verses is that today the Lord is omnipresent because He is the Spirit, and He is not only within the believers, but He is waiting for the unbelievers at their mouth. If they would exercise their mouth to call Him "Lord Jesus," they will make a real transaction with the Lord.

We need to learn all these things in order to make a living transaction. We should not talk too much. We simply need to convince someone, open his understanding, and incline his heart a little. Then when we realize that he is more or less convinced, we should not speak any more. We should simply say, "Let us pray." He may say, "I don't know how to pray," so we can tell him to call on the Lord Jesus with his mouth and from his heart. In this way we help him to make a real transaction with the Lord. Then after he prays, we must help him to realize that to believe in the Lord Jesus is not to receive a religion. In order to receive a religion, one must learn many things, such as regulations, doctrines, teachings, philosophies, and performances. Rather, we should tell him, "You are receiving and dealing with a living One, who is the very God of the universe in the person of the Son, the living Christ who gives life. Today this living Christ is the living Spirit. He is waiting here, so since you prayed and called on His name, He is within you. Now He is always within you. The only thing you must do now is take care of the inner sense of life." I have done this many times. It is very easy, but we must experience all these things, and we must study the Word.

For this purpose, we must learn to use the Scriptures in a living way. We may compare using the Scriptures to serving chicken. In the Scriptures there are many matters, some of which are like the feathers. A chicken needs feathers to grow well, but when we help people, we should not minister the "feathers." We must know which part we need to minister to others as life. We must learn how to use the proper verses.

PUTTING THESE MATTERS INTO PRACTICE IN A LIVING WAY

We should promise the Lord that we will bring one person to Him each year. We may even sign and date a piece of paper to this effect. This will help us. If we do this, we can be assured that we will bring one or two persons to the Lord, but if we do not make such a promise, we may not bring one person to the Lord even in two years. I do not like to force anyone, but I am concerned, especially for the young brothers and sisters. The more I pray, minister, and teach as one of the Lord's servants, the more I have learned not to put my trust in people; we are just not trustworthy. Therefore, as I have been speaking about the outreach, I consider whether or not the young ones will put this into practice. What will be the help if all this training becomes mere talk? Some may say that we should let the Holy Spirit do the work. The Holy Spirit will do His work, but we have to cooperate. When we are cooking, have we ever said, "I have to pray and let the Holy Spirit start the fire"? It is we, not the Holy Spirit, that starts the fire. I look to the Lord that after the young brothers and sisters receive this training, they would put it into practice.

In the past when I held trainings with the young people in

the Far East, I told them that if they truly meant business to be trained, they should sign a paper saying that they accept all the regulations and rules of the training. After they signed, I treated them strictly as trainees. I gave them some assignments, and they did them. This truly helped them. In the same principle, we should put all the matters about which we have been speaking into practice. If we do not, they will mean little to us. The young brothers and sisters should do some "homework" on the matter of life. They can go to a concordance or another kind of help to select all the best passages concerning life. Then they should read, meditate, and consider them, try to use them, and check themselves as to whether or not they have the experience they speak about. They should deal with the Lord, learn these things, and try to experience these things. Then they should also keep their word before the Lord. They should say, "Lord, I have the burden, and I have told You that within one year I will bring at least one person to You." When they pray about this and put it into practice, they will be burdened to care for two or three particular persons. Then to be sure, some persons will be brought in.

We have been influenced too much, even spoiled, by the background of Christianity. We must make a turn and start to preach the gospel in a new way. Then all the new ones who are brought in will go on in the same way that we practice. If we do not do this, we will have the old way of gospel preaching through a minister, preacher, evangelist, or campaign, not through the living members of the Body. The best way for the gospel to be preached is day by day through the living members. Then after a certain time, perhaps one or two months, the church will need to have a baptism, because ten, twenty, or even forty people will be ready. When more new ones are saved, the church will have another baptism. This is the right way.

Whether or not we have this turn depends on us. We must practice this living way of preaching the gospel. I hope that we will bring these matters to the Lord and make a decision before Him to put them into practice. We should not make excuses. We can always gain someone. When D. L. Moody was young, he made the decision to preach the gospel to at least one person each day. Once after he had gone to bed, he realized that he had not preached the gospel that day, so he rose, dressed again, and went out to the street. He could not find anyone, but eventually he saw a policeman and told him, "Sir, you must believe in Jesus." The policeman was bothered but impressed. The next day he found out about Moody and went to talk with him, and eventually he was saved. There are many "policemen" on the streets. We should go there and catch them.

ABOUT THE AUTHOR

Witness Lee was born in 1905 in northern China and raised in a Christian family. At age 19 he was fully captured for Christ and immediately consecrated himself to preach the gospel for the rest of his life. Early in his service, he met Watchman Nee, a renowned preacher, teacher, and writer. Witness Lee labored together with Watchman Nee under his direction. In 1934 Watchman Nee entrusted Witness Lee with the responsibility for his publication operation, called the Shanghai Gospel Bookroom.

Prior to the Communist takeover in 1949, Witness Lee was sent by Watchman Nee and his other co-workers to Taiwan to insure that the things delivered to them by the Lord would not be lost. Watchman Nee instructed Witness Lee to continue the former's publishing operation abroad as the Taiwan Gospel Bookroom, which has been publicly recognized as the publisher of Watchman Nee's works outside China. Witness Lee's work in Taiwan manifested the Lord's abundant blessing. From a mere 350 believers, newly fled from the mainland, the churches in Taiwan grew to 20,000 in five years.

In 1962 Witness Lee felt led of the Lord to come to the United States, settling in California. During his 35 years of service in the U.S., he ministered in weekly meetings and weekend conferences, delivering several thousand spoken messages. Much of his speaking has since been published as over 400 titles. Many of these have been translated into over fourteen languages. He gave his last public conference in February 1997 at the age of 91.

He leaves behind a prolific presentation of the truth in the Bible. His major work, *Life-study of the Bible,* comprises over 25,000 pages of commentary on every book of the Bible from the perspective of the believers' enjoyment and experience of God's divine life in Christ through the Holy Spirit. Witness Lee was the chief editor of a new translation of the New Testament into Chinese called the Recovery Version and directed the translation of the same into English. The Recovery Version also appears in a number of other languages. He provided an extensive body of footnotes, outlines, and spiritual cross references. A radio broadcast of his messages can be heard on Christian radio stations in the United States. In 1965 Witness Lee founded Living Stream Ministry, a non-profit corporation, located in Anaheim, California, which officially presents his and Watchman Nee's ministry.

Witness Lee's ministry emphasizes the experience of Christ as life and the practical oneness of the believers as the Body of Christ. Stressing the importance of attending to both these matters, he led the churches under his care to grow in Christian life and function. He was unbending in his conviction that God's goal is not narrow sectarianism but the Body of Christ. In time, believers began to meet simply as the church in their localities in response to this conviction. In recent years a number of new churches have been raised up in Russia and in many eastern European countries.

OTHER BOOKS PUBLISHED BY
Living Stream Ministry

Available at
Christian bookstores, or contact Living Stream Ministry
2431 W. La Palma Ave. • Anaheim, CA 92801
1-800-549-5164 • www.livingstream.com